"If we can start this movement, I think it will be possible, through education and awareness, to bring an end to war. What is the use of war? It brings destruction, more suffering, and pain. I believe that humans have common sense, and that human basic nature is more compassionate. Please inform people how serious war and the killing of human beings is. Please also share that the use of this weaponry creates tremendous destruction. It is a total waste of money. .... This has been one of my dreams for a number of years."

HH the Dalai Lama in conversation with Scilla Elworthy,
Mind and Life Conference, September 2016

"In this extraordinary and surprising book Scilla Elworthy dissects the Big Picture: Why do wars happen? What is the real damage? Who gains from them? What would peace entail and how do we achieve it? What's the good news? These are some of the most difficult and essential questions of our time. Scilla tackles them with grace, generosity and a wealth of experience, offering examples and proposals for new and peaceful ways of conceptualising the human future. This is a compact book with an enormous message. Please read it."

Brian Eno, lifelong pioneer in rock, ambient and electronic music

---

"I find it impossible to comprehend how so many of the human race seem more intent on waging wanton destruction, rather than creating sustainable solutions towards establishing lasting peace. This is why Scilla Elworthy's exceptional book is so compelling. It has been written for people who want to step out of helplessness and find out how they can apply their own personal skills to do something about the challenges now facing us. Read on and learn how you can engage."

Annie Lennox OBE, singer, songwriter, political activist and philanthropist

"Scared by what they see on TV — a world of crisis and confusion — young people constantly ask Scilla Elworthy "what can I do?" She shows us what is already effective in building peace at both local and international levels, and how minimal is the cost compared to the costs of fighting wars. She confirms the massive impact that ordinary people can have in making a peaceful world possible, and how they can do it. Read this book and help create the peaceful world we all want to live in."

David Hartsough, Co-founder of World Beyond War and the Nonviolent Peaceforce, nominated for the Nobel Peace Prize

---

"This book is timely, well-informed, authoritative and readable. It challenges my assumptions about the inevitability of armed conflict, and calls on us to review beliefs that may have been unquestioned hitherto. It offers a clear and compelling case for the practicalities of building a more peaceful world, and calls for a culture change in how we manage conflict. It is highly practical on a personal as well as a global level, with clear suggestions for actions that we can take e.g. steps to disseminate these ideas to government and media. By assembling 'known and viable initiatives' Scilla Elworthy has given me a sense of hope that so many organisations world-wide are taking positive steps in peace-building."

Lawrence Kershen, Chair, Search for Common Ground UK, former Chair, Restorative Justice Council

---

"For all of us working to build a more just and peaceful world, this book provides not only the inspiration but also the evidence we've been looking for. As Dr. Elworthy eloquently explains, military options are no longer viable in today's world. We must find nonviolent solutions to the problems we face; peacebuilding is both practical and effective."

Bridget Moix, Clerk of the Board, Friends Committee on National Legislation, USA

"War is a complicated matter. At last Scilla Elworthy has simplified the horrific financial costs together with toolkits, advice and examples for effective prevention of conflict. War has passed its sell-by date, and in this easy to read book the author clearly demonstrates why."

Lawrence Bloom, former Chair of the World Economic Forum, Global Agenda Council

---

"This remarkable and deeply timely book is of the highest relevance for anyone, in any walk of life, who has the desire to contribute to creating a better world. Drawing on her decades of experience of dialogue and working with global decision-makers, Dr Elworthy brings together a wide-ranging framework of strategic actions with the inner disciplines needed to make them more effective as well as to build personal resilience. She has researched and created what must be the first, and therefore landmark, detailed financial model for the creation of peace initiatives worldwide. Highly readable, practical and peppered with pithy and often moving true stories, this is truly a unique and essential book for our time."

Nicholas Janni, Founder, Core Presence; Co-Founder, Vessica

"Finally, what we have known intuitively is now demonstrated in plain English utilizing business principles. A business plan for peace resonates with me as it will with thousands of Rotarians worldwide. Dr Elworthy's work is groundbreaking and hopeful. Imagine giving up war which costs US$1,600,000,000,000 dollars per year with unimaginable side effects for a mere two hundred million dollars per year. This is a must read."

Al Jubitz, Founding President of the Rotarian Action Group for Peace; Founder of the War Prevention Initiative

"It is no longer adequate to simply be non-discriminatory. To make the kind of change needed and to end war, people have to be "actively inclusive". Scilla is showing that we have the tools and has given us a blueprint for maximizing our potential."

Daniel Danso, *Global Diversity Expert, Linklaters*

"This is a very powerful book that faces head-on the appalling cost of war but goes far beyond this. Scilla Elworthy does not just argue persuasively that war should be seen as obsolete but she shows how we can control and reverse our culture of militarism. She does this through a series of chapters that take us from the international and national through to the local and the personal. The Business Plan for Peace achieves the remarkable feat of combining realism with optimism – a singularly powerful antidote to the despair that can so readily come from facing up to the problem of violence."

Paul Rogers, *Emeritus Professor of Peace Studies, Bradford University*

"The Business Plan for Peace has the power to transform the collective mind set. How can we seriously deal with warriors, populists, terrorists and extremists and meet the growing security needs of citizens? With this book, Scilla demonstrates the avant-garde of peace activists and motivates couch-potatoes like me as well. Although it's written for millennials, we may all learn from a great wise woman how to build a world that works for all."

Kerstin Löber, *Psychological Safety Expert for DAX 100 companies in Germany, co-founder of FemmeQ*

THE BUSINESS PLAN FOR PEACE

Building a World Without War

DR SCILLA ELWORTHY

Published by
Peace Direct
First Floor,
1 King Edward's Road,
London E9 7SF
UK

Cover photo © by Pal Hansen
Photographs by Maggie Nielson, Corrie Wingate, Fronteiras do
Pensamento, Jordi Bernabeu Farrús, Claude Truong-Ngoc

Design by Ben Shmulevitch

Set in Lexia, Dalton Maag

ISBN: 978–1–999–81640–7

WORLD
LAND
TRUST™

www.carbonbalancedpaper.com
CBP000123542404154100

This book is dedicated with love and respect to my mentor, guide and friend, Professor Adam Curle [1916–2006] — a most profound practitioner in the prevention of war.

"Support courage where there is fear, foster agreement where there is conflict, and inspire hope where there is despair."

Nelson Mandela, *as Founder of The Elders at the Launch, 2007*

WHY THIS BOOK?

We live in a world in crisis. Those who are even half awake realise this, but many feel helpless and powerless and shut down in face of what they see on TV or read in the news. This book is for all those who want to step out of helplessness and find out how they can apply their own personal skills to do something about the challenges now facing us.

It is for the millions of people who are now so horrified by what they have seen of war since the turn of the century that they want to act, they want to do something to stop this tsunami of suffering. They are asking — at every event, conference, broadcast, or online course — "what can I do?" This is an upsurge of passionate commitment noticed by all my colleagues.

At the same time our inboxes are packed daily with examples of what people ARE doing, informing us about what works and what doesn't. Often it's the people closest to crisis — to armed violence, to the horrors faced by refugees, to the fallout of global warming — that are coming up with the best strategies.

So this book will first investigate the forces that drive armed violence, because that information is essential if those drivers are to be curbed. I will then show what is already working to build peace effectively at both local and international levels. I shall demonstrate what it would cost to scale up those systems that work best, so for the first time ever we can estimate a costed Business Plan for Peace. Finally I shall reveal the massive impact that ordinary people can now have in making a peaceful world possible.

After all, it has now become a life or death question for all of us, and for our children and children's children.

Obviously there are tomes to be written on these subjects, but the people I want to reach don't have time to read long academic analyses. So I have kept the facts and arguments in each case to a few — and you will know many more. I've also wanted to include the human side of things — the mistakes I have made, what a crisis felt like at the time, the incredible warmth and courage of the people I've been lucky enough to work with, and the times when it has been nourishing and inspiring and even a lot of fun.

WHAT WE FACE

The work I do has involved me with people who seem to have a lot of power — physicists who design nuclear warheads, military officers in charge of nuclear weapons, manufacturers who produce and sell missiles and machine guns, strategists who design defence policies, as well as those who sign the cheques — not just in Britain but in America, Russia, France, China, Israel, India and Pakistan. I also now work with people who risk their lives to stop other people being killed by these weapons, trying their best to build peaceful societies. I spend a lot of time listening to all these people.

For many people peace can seem boring — too well behaved, too quiet. These are usually the people who have never been in a war, never witnessed the terror of children watching their parents tortured, never seen a human skull exploding, never heard the screams of a grandfather trapped under concrete beams, never looked into the eyes of a woman who has been multiply raped.

The wounds of war take three generations to heal — at a minimum. Some are not healed even after seven centuries. Even a 'minimal' action taken in war, for example one sniper squeezing a trigger — a decision of a millisecond — will kill an innocent baker and send an entire family into destitution on the streets.

At this point in history, I am strongly aware that humanity has built up looming threats to our security that weaponry cannot even begin to deal with — climate change, the rich-poor divide, migration, over population, terrorism. Therefore it is time to take a hard look at both the military—industrial complex that drives war, and others for whom war means wealth. It is time to divert their skills and our skills to making what humanity now needs. It's time to access a better kind of intelligence, to demonstrate how conflicts can be prevented and resolved without armed violence. It is time to build a Business Plan for Peace and to make peace profitable.

WHAT MOTIVATED ME TO WRITE

I come from a military family. My father fought in the artillery in the First World War, my eldest brother was a paratrooper, my third brother was in the Royal Navy and was killed when I was ten years old. I learned to shoot with a gun at 11, to fly aeroplanes at 26, and to parachute at 40. In Bosnia I sat at the bedside of a man whose eyes had been destroyed by a sniper's bullet. In the Congo I quailed before the crazed terror of armed and drunken soldiers out of control. In Japan I watched the faces of those who saw at first hand the untold horrors of the atomic explosion in Hiroshima.

Later however, I learned how a young woman in northern Pakistan convinces young jihadis not to become suicide bombers. I got to know a former child soldier in the Congo who now rescues children kidnapped by militias, and brings them home. I witnessed the growing reconciliation between the Brighton bomber and the daughter of the man he killed. I watched how a network of rural women stopped electoral violence in Zimbabwe. I had the great privilege of observing at first hand the peace — making skills of Desmond Tutu, Mary Robinson and Graca Machel in the development of The Elders. When Nelson Mandela launched

The Elders in 2007 he said: "Using their collective experience, their moral courage and their ability to rise above the parochial concerns of nation, race and creed, they can help make our planet a more peaceful, healthy and equitable place to live."

What I have seen of war, and the building of peace, convinces me that human beings are well able to find better ways to resolve conflict than by killing each other. It's not easy, but we now know how to do it. This short book is a first attempt to answer some of the tough questions involved. It is by no means complete or comprehensive, and your improvements and ideas will be welcome.

Doing this work the key thing I have learned is that power — even the power to blow up the world or not blow it up — is not some huge unreachable monolith. Power is simply human beings making decisions, in some cases human beings convinced by the seductive idea that ultimate power brings ultimate security. But they are still just people — people with stomach upsets and beloved children and heartaches, and whose cars even break down sometimes. And if they are just people then it is possible to communicate with them, as people.

CONTENTS

The book is designed to work in three parts: the first outlines the current context of war and the drivers of war; the second investigates how war can be stopped, and what it will cost to do so; the third suggests the kind of actions that any individual can contribute to the building of peace.

INTRODUCTION

In 2003, shortly after the invasion of Iraq, US Lieutenant Colonel Chris Hughes was leading his men down a street in Najaf, when suddenly people came pouring out of the houses lining the street, surrounding the troops. These local people were furiously angry, screaming, and waving their fists. The heavily armed soldiers, most of them still in their teens and speaking no Arabic, had no idea what was happening. Chris Hughes strode into the middle of the crowd, raised his rifle above his head, pointed the barrel at the ground, and shouted an order to his men that they had never heard before: "Kneel". The bewildered troops, burdened by their heavy body armour, wobbled to the ground and pointed their rifles into the sand. The crowd quieted in disbelief, and there was absolute stillness for some two minutes. And then the crowd dispersed.[1] This gesture of respect averted a bloodbath; no-one was killed, no weapons were needed, no shots were fired, no revenge was required.

This true story demonstrates two clues to stopping war. The first is that humiliation is a key driver of violence, and respect is the strongest antidote to humiliation. It is also the fastest way to calm a conflict. The second is the presence of mind shown by Lt Colonel Hughes; he saw in a millisecond that a massacre was about to happen, and was sufficiently present to know instantly what was necessary. It is this quality of awareness combined with wisdom that can change the course of history. My hope is that this book may help us all to develop similar qualities.

People feel helpless in face of the enormity of war. Syrian cities entirely reduced to rubble, terrified people fleeing barrel bombs and chlorine attacks, endless columns of massive tanks pounding their way into new territory, unidentifiable fighter planes screaming overhead, girls of ten auctioned to warlords who rape them so viciously that they die.

What we hope to begin in this book, for others to improve, is to offer ways in which the very evident upsurge of popular will to end war can find traction. To do this it is vital to understand the forces that drive war, and why wars continue. In chapter one we investigate the costs of war compared to what is currently spent on building peace, and ask if war is actually inevitable. Chapter two examines the business that is war, and how lucrative is the trafficking that thrives in the chaos of destroyed societies. Since we're curious to understand motives, we shall also dare to ask why people fight.

Chapter three opens the question of how war can be stopped. To have any hope of doing this, we clearly need to understand how policy-makers think, and why they act on certain assumptions.

It is important to make a distinction between war and conflict. Conflict in the sense of argument or disagreement is neither good nor bad, it is simply energy, and as such a part of human experience. War has certainly been for centuries a part of human experience, but the assertion in this book is that war is no longer necessary. We now know enough to make wiser decisions and implement them, and save trillions of dollars that can be used to alleviate suffering, educate, feed and bring water to tens of millions of people, and help the earth to re-generate.

So in chapter four we begin to get granular, and examine the basic strategies for building peace. Such strategies are based on newer assumptions than those that currently underpin our addiction to killing.

We examine what can be done at local levels, as well as at national and international levels. We demonstrate what policy makers, business people and manufacturers can do to enable peace to take the place of war as a source of profit. In chapter five we make the first attempt to cost such a plan.

At the beginning of chapter six there is a reframing of the same content and vision, but now exploring the question of how, and how fast, humanity is evolving toward a far more awakened, empathic society — even in the context of ongoing violence. We examine the remarkable rise in citizen readiness to act across cultures to build peaceful environments and prevent violence.

Note to reader: you may wonder about the use of the word 'we' in this book. If at times the 'we' seems to be geared to a western audience this is a fair observation. Within this 'we' lies the acknowledgement that western countries lead the majority of global military expenditure. And therefore this 'we' emphasises the necessity for these countries to initiate a major shift in policy and divestment as a condition to create peace.

Then we come closer to home, to respond to the questions that all these people are asking: we spell out what 'ordinary' people can do to prevent armed violence in their communities, in their nations and internationally.

Chapter eight is, in many ways, the most vital chapter in the book. It addresses the personal work — the inner development — that is essential if people are to be effective in their efforts to make the world a safer place. This is for a specific reason: when we have strong emotions like fear or anger, if we're not awake to what's going on inside us, we tend to 'project' those emotions onto others.

This 'projection', on a larger scale, is what causes wars. Leaders become excessively incensed with the aggressivity of the other side when they have not examined and dealt with their own internal anger, which may even date back to childhood. This demonisation of the other permits all kinds of horrors.

3

If we are to work effectively in conflict, whether in government or at the grassroots, we need to understand this kind of projection on a personal level. To do this can be uncomfortable and can require real courage, because we are confronting our own deeply embedded convictions and emotions. But when we really get it — that is, really get what a hugely powerful force it can be — we become ten times more effective.

The Toolbox at the end of the book provides some answers to the question of "How do I do this?" It contains trusted exercises to develop the skills that people need to acquire to turn themselves into inspiring builders of peaceful societies.

What becomes evident in this work is that we are living through an age of profound transformation in the human condition. The man-made issues we face in this turbulent age are challenging our human capacity to evolve. We have the opportunity now, as never before, to develop our consciousness — and therefore our way of treating one another — to a new level.

PART ONE: THE PROBLEM OF WAR

Chapter 1

Why it is in Global Interests to Stop War

This chapter briefly describes the vast amounts of money and resources wasted in war, as well as the absence of accountability and the longer-term problems caused by war — including psychological damage that can last for generations, as well as the physical damage to people and eco-systems. The unintended consequences of war, almost never taken into account when wars are declared, include the humiliation and marginalisation of whole peoples, obviously leading to the rise of terrorism.

War creates long-term problems — centuries of revenge, terrorism, floods of refugees, children maimed for life

The tragedy and chaos that is Syria is but one example of the profound — often invisible — damage that is done when armed conflict replaces any form of negotiation. In March 2011, after four decades of dictatorship, the Syrian people rose up peacefully to demand freedom and dignity. The regime of Bashar al-Assad crushed that uprising with force, triggering an international war that has killed more than 470,000 and driven at least 12 million people[2] — half of Syria's population — from their homes.

With the involvement of Iran, Saudi Arabia, the Gulf Emirates, Turkey and Russia as well as a US-led coalition, Syria's complex war has become a battleground for geopolitical rivalry. In the rubble of this destruction extremists like Daesh and Jabhat al-Nusra have flourished.

UNICEF says that the ongoing conflict in Syria has caused the largest humanitarian crisis since the Second World War, with the lives of more than 8 million children in danger.[3] Every day, Syrian children face unspeakable violence, endless nights and days of terror, a lack of food, and increased disease. If they are not killed or maimed by barrel bombs, if they do not die for lack of medical care, they are subject to exploitation and abuse, early marriage, child labour and recruitment by armed groups. The scale of the crisis for children is unprecedented. At the end of chapter five, in order to learn from this tragedy, we shall try to examine how the deep pain and suffering of the Syrian war might have been prevented.

Violence costs vast amounts; building peace is totally underfunded

"The 2016 Global Peace Index report found that the economic impact of all violence (including the military, homicide, incarceration, policing etc) to the global economy was $13.6 trillion in 2015, equivalent to $5 *per day* for every person on the planet."[4]

$13,600,000,000,000

This figure is simply staggering. It took me several tries to get the number of zeros correct.

The Institute for Economics and Peace, which works with the Economist Intelligence Unit to produce the Global Peace Index, continues: "These numbers are notable for two reasons. Firstly, over 70 per cent of the economic impact of violence accrues from what is mostly government spending on the military and internal security. This shows that significant amounts of government expenditure are tied up to this end. In a peaceful world, these huge resources would be directed elsewhere. Secondly, the remaining amount is consequential losses from violence and conflict and these, too, are enormous. They significantly outweigh the international community's spending on building peace."

A quick examination of the numbers reveals that the world continues to spend vastly disproportionate resources on creating and containing violence compared to what it spends on peace. In 2015 alone, UN peacekeeping expenditures of $8.27 billion totalled only 1.1 per cent of the estimated economic losses from armed conflict.

Peace-building expenditures are aimed at developing and maintaining the capacities for resilience to armed conflict, whereas peacekeeping operations are a response once a conflict has erupted. The former aims to reduce the risk of lapsing or relapsing into violent conflict by strengthening national capacities and institutions for conflict prevention and laying the foundations of sustainable peace and development. The chart below shows that the spending in 2015 on peace-building ($6.8 billion) and peacekeeping ($8.27 billion) together represent just 2 per cent of the economic losses caused by conflict. These numbers demonstrate a serious under-investment in the activities that build peace and show how the international community is spending too much on conflict and too little on peace. Given the fact that the cost of violence is so significant, the economic argument for more spending on peace is powerful.[5]

Global Value, 2015 ($Billions)

Figures from Institute for Economics & Peace, 2016[6]

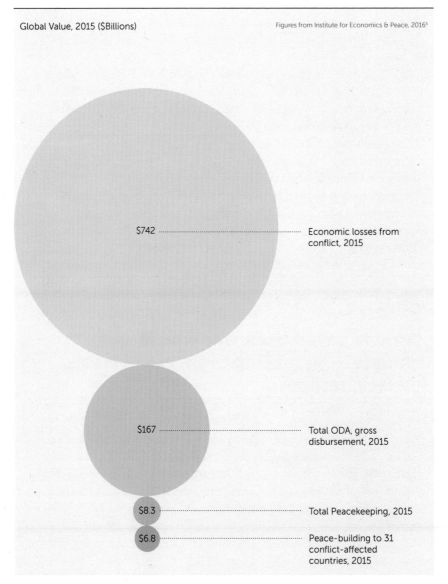

$742 — Economic losses from conflict, 2015

$167 — Total ODA, gross disbursement, 2015

$8.3 — Total Peacekeeping, 2015

$6.8 — Peace-building to 31 conflict-affected countries, 2015

Extraordinary sums disappear without trace in the military

One example of many: the US Department of Defence Inspector General's report, released August 2016, left Americans stunned at the jaw-dropping lack of accountability and oversight. The report revealed the Pentagon could not account for $6.5 trillion dollars worth of Army general fund transactions and data, according to a report by the Fiscal Times.

The Pentagon has apparently never completed an audit that would reveal how the agency has specifically spent the trillions of dollars allocated to them by Congress for wars, equipment, personnel, housing, healthcare and procurement.

Since 1996 all federal agencies have been mandated by law to conduct regular financial audits. However, the Pentagon has NEVER complied with that federal law. In 20 years, it has never accounted for the trillions of dollars in taxpayer funds it has spent, in part because "fudging" the numbers has become standard operating procedure at the Department of Defence, as revealed in a 2013 Reuters investigation by Scot Paltrow.

Adding to the appearance of impropriety is the fact that thousands of documents that should be on file have been removed and disappeared without any reasonable explanation.[7]

Money saved from war would save people — providing food, clean water, safety, refuge...

World Beyond War is a global nonviolent movement to end war and establish a just and sustainable peace. They calculate that it would cost about $30 billion per year to end starvation and hunger around the world, and about $11 billion per year to provide the world with clean water. What if another $450 billion went into providing the world with green energy and infrastructure, topsoil preservation, environmental protection, schools, medicine, programs of cultural exchange, and the study of peace and of nonviolent action?

Figures from World Beyond War

Global yearly spending on war: **$2 trillion**

United States yearly spending on war: **$1 trillion**

Cost to end starvation around the world: **$30 billion** [159]

"Every year, the world spends about $2 trillion on wars and — primarily — on the preparation for wars. The United States spends about half of that, about $1 trillion, through various departments including the military, state, energy, homeland security, central intelligence agency, etc. Over half of the rest of the world's military spending is by the United States' close allies, and a huge chunk is foreign purchases from US corporations. Ceasing to fund militarism would save a great many lives and halt the counterproductive work of antagonizing the world and generating enemies. [Moreover] moving even a fraction of that money into useful places would save many times that number of lives and begin generating friendship instead of animosity."[8]

Militarism cannot address future threats — climate change, migration, water shortage, rich-poor gap...

Polling by the Pew Research Centre in 2015 in 40 countries around the world indicated that the global public are more concerned about climate change than any other 'threat' — from a list that also included ISIS, economic instability, and the bellicosity of Russia, Iran or China.[9]

Climate change is causing the disappearance of grazing lands, floods, resource scarcity and the mass displacement of peoples.

- The percentage of land affected by serious drought has doubled from the 1970s to the early 2000s. About half of our planet's agricultural land is moderately or severely degraded.[10] Therefore about 50,000,000 people may be forced to seek new homes and livelihoods within only 10 years.[11]
- In 50 years, a single lifetime, the earth has been more radically changed than by ALL previous generations of humanity.

Water shortage

- The UN 2016 Water Report claims that 1.8 billion people have no "reliable access" to water deemed "safe for human consumption."[12] Producing 1 kilo of beef requires about 15,000 litres of water.
- 33 countries will face "extremely high water stress" in less than 25 years.[13]

Marginalisation of the vast majority of the world's population

- Oxfam claims in its January 2017 inequality report, that "over the last 30 years the growth in the incomes of the bottom 50% has been zero, whereas incomes of the top 1% have grown 300%." This means that now "eight men now own the same amount of wealth as the poorest half of the world."[14]
- The average European cow gets a subsidy of $2 a day (the *World Bank measure of poverty*); more than half of the people in the developing world live on less than that. "It appears that it is better to be a cow in Europe than to be a poor person in a developing country." [15]

Global inequality is growing so fast that it will fuel further terror groups and revolutionary movements

The poorest half of the world population owns as much as a small group of the global super-rich — so small, you would fit them all on a single coach. Runaway inequality has created a world where these 8 people own as much as the poorest half of the world's population.

Nobel Prize-winning economist Joseph Stiglitz says: "...free trade has not worked because we have not tried it: trade agreements of the past have been neither free nor fair. They have been asymmetric, opening up markets in the developing countries to goods from the advanced industrial countries without full reciprocation. A host of subtle but effective trade barriers has been kept in place. This asymmetric globalisation has put developing countries at a disadvantage. It has left them worse off than they would be with a truly free and fair trade regime."[16]

Moreover, the rich/poor gap is widening each year, signalling that richer cultures simply do not care about poverty. This lack of respect is not only humiliating, but has become one of the chief triggers of resentment leading to revolutionary movements and then terrorism.

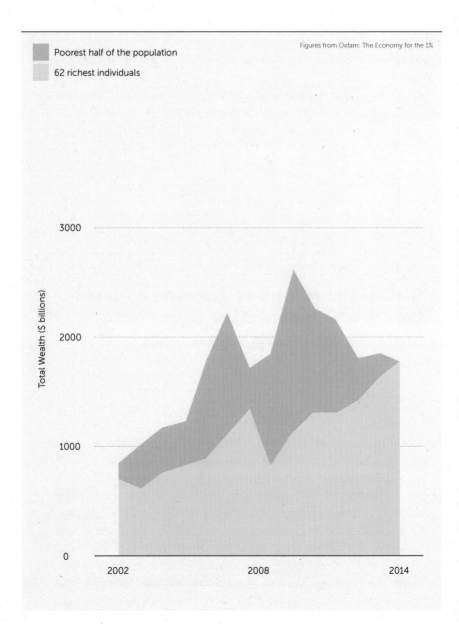

Poorest half of the population

62 richest individuals

Figures from Oxfam: The Economy for the 1%

Total Wealth ($ billions)

3000

2000

1000

0

2002   2008   2014

Rape as a weapon of war

Human Rights Watch investigators have concluded that rape as 'a weapon of war is used by all sides to deliberately terrorise civilians, to exert control over them, or to punish them for perceived collaboration with the enemy.' Rape of women and children is widely used by soldiers not only to 'punish' the other side, but because they feel they have the right to take out their fury and lust on the most vulnerable human bodies available. After raping a woman, a stick or knife is often inserted into the vagina to deliberately cause a hole between the vagina and rectum or bladder, meaning that the woman will then dribble urine or excreta for the rest of her life.[17] This condition is known as fistula.

The result of rape as a weapon of war is to extend post-conflict chaos because the children born have no idea who is their father; moreover the anguish of a woman who has given birth to a child whose father is the 'enemy' can only be imagined.

The authors of the report by Human Rights Watch[18] say that rape victims in the Congo claim that the war is being fought 'on their bodies' and they conclude that the scale of sexual violence in the eastern Congo makes the area the most dangerous place on earth to be a woman.[19]

Is the world becoming more violent?

The Global Peace Index from the Institute for Economics and Peace shows that peace over the past eight years has had two distinct and divergent trends: in 2014 Europe continued long-term trends of improvement as homicide rates and interpersonal violence continue to drop to record lows. Concurrently, escalating civil war and steep rises in terrorism in the Middle East have caused severe deteriorations in peace in the region.

"Trends show that the distribution of peace across the globe is mirroring wealth: peaceful countries are becoming more peaceful while the most violent are becoming more violent. Considering that more than two billion people live in the 20 least peaceful countries in the world, the net effect of this widening peace gap is disproportionately skewed to the negative. Whether you believe the world is more peaceful depends on your frame of reference and statistical choices."[20]

Quietly over the last 15 years, many African wars did end. Lingering Cold War struggles like the Angolan civil war burned out. West African nations including Liberia and Sierra Leone ceased being playgrounds for warlords and regained their status as functional, if weak, states. Eastern Congo is still violent, but far less so than during the 1990s 'African World War'. Overall, 21st-century Africa has seen more wars end or abate than ignite.[21]

Is war inevitable?

"We have changed everything save our mode of thinking and thus we drift towards unparalleled catastrophes."
— Albert Einstein, 24 May 1946

The past century has seen some of the most terrifying and destructive wars in human history, but it has also, for the first time in human history, seen the greatest achievements in co-operation — witness the European Union and the United Nations — as well the greatest advances in expertise on the prevention and resolution of conflict.

The latest knowledge, experience and training for the prevention and resolution of conflict are available in multiple locations, including the Peace-making and Conflict Prevention Programme at UNITAR,[22] the network of field operations and the Conflict Prevention Centre at OSCE,[23] the Women in Security, Conflict Management and Peace, a pioneering peace-building initiative in South Asia, and many others.

About 400 colleges and universities around the world offer peace studies programmes, and notable research institutes like the Stockholm International Peace Research Institute offer multiple databases, such as the SIPRI Multilateral Peace Operations Database, giving information on all peace operations conducted since 2000.

So the knowledge of how to prevent war and resolve conflict is substantial, and training is fully available. As humans we are no longer obliged to repeat the deadly cycle of atrocity, terror, grief, anger, revenge and retaliation. We know enough not to do this any more. We have better methods of preventing people killing each other.

War is past its sell-by date.

Chapter 2

The Drivers of War

War is driven by aggression, greed, fanaticism, ambition, fear or threat. When I interviewed senior British nuclear weapons decision-makers in the late 1980s, for 93 per cent of them the fundamental reason for the UK to possess nuclear weapons was to deter the threat from another nation. The spectre of another nation building up an arsenal and using belligerent language tends to provoke an equal and opposite reaction.

Until now it has been normal to consider military might as the determinant of an international pecking order. Possession of the weapons and the forces to deter or frighten other nations has even determined the structure of the United Nations, giving the power of veto to the five Permanent Members of the Security Council. The effect of this has been, as in Syria, to make the UN impotent to stop the massacre of civilians.

The UK has been at war somewhere, with someone, since the Second World War ended. The list of our wars and military operations is a long one including India, Palestine, Malaya, Korea, Suez Canal Zone, Kenya, Cyprus, Suez 1956, Borneo, Vietnam, Aden, Radfan, Oman, Dhofar, Northern Ireland, the Falklands War, Bosnia, Kosovo, the Gulf War, Afghanistan, Sierra Leone, Iraq and Libya.

War makes a few people extremely rich, and serves the interests of corporations, governments and strategists

In 2013 the US military budget was higher than the nine other biggest military budgets in the world combined. Here's one example of how this happens:

Lockheed Martin, in partnership with BAE Systems, is building the F-35 Joint Strike Fighter, likely to be the largest programme in the history of military aviation. Originally approved by Congress with a promised price tag of $62 million per aircraft, that price had risen by 81 per cent to $111 million over a few years. In August 2013 the Congressional Quarterly and the Government Accountability Office were indicating the "total estimated program cost now is $400 billion, nearly twice the initial cost".

Nations by Military Expenditure in 2015

Figures from Stockholm International Peace Institute

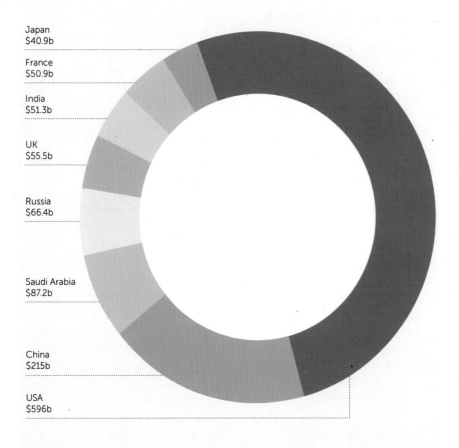

Japan
$40.9b

France
$50.9b

India
$51.3b

UK
$55.5b

Russia
$66.4b

Saudi Arabia
$87.2b

China
$215b

USA
$596b

Global military expenditure rose in 2016 to $1686 billion. That is $1,686,000,000,000.[24] This figure makes me gasp, because according to the United Nations it would cost $340,000,000,000 per year to provide primary and secondary education to every child in the world[25] and $28,400,000,000 per year to provide universal basic water and sanitation services by 2030[26]. There would then be an ample $1,317,600,000,000 left over per year to address all the other Sustainable Development Goals, and still allow nations to defend themselves.

This figure also represents a 64.2% increase in global military expenditure from 1999–2016.[27] If this increase alone had been spent on dealing with the causes of armed conflict and preventing wars breaking out, we would have a very different world today.

Andrew Feinstein has analysed the international arms market with a unique level of detail. He reports: "In our twenty first century the lethal combination of technological advances, terrorism, global crime, state — sponsored violence and socio-economic inequality has raised instability and insecurity to alarming levels. At the same time, the engine that has driven this escalation, the global arms trade, grows ever more sophisticated, complex and toxic in its effects ... It operates according to its own rules, largely un-scrutinised, bringing enormous benefits to the chosen few, and suffering to millions. The trade corrodes our democracies, weakens already fragile states and often undermines the very security it purports to strengthen."[28]

Those who thrive in war are not only arms manufacturers but also people traffickers, arms smugglers, money launderers, drug dealers — and others who require a lawless environment to make a fortune.

The crisis in Darfur has been called the first genocide of the 21st century. There have been many explanations offered for this human tragedy but what is often overlooked is the economic value of violence for the Sudanese State and the Janjaweed militia. The discovery of gold in Northern Darfur in an area called Jebel Amer has meant that in 2013, 70,000 people were removed to leave the land open to gold speculators and mining agents. The notorious Janjaweed Leader Musa Hilal then installed himself in Jebel Amer and is reputed to be personally earning $54 million per year from gold. A UN Security Council Panel of Experts' Report in April 2016 claims that $123 million from gold extraction is now fuelling the violence in Darfur.[29]

The global arms trade fuels war, remains secret and is unregulated

It is estimated that the total value of the global arms trade in 2014 was at least $94.5 billion. By contrast, just $10 billion would cover the cost of bringing clean water and sanitation to everyone on the planet.[30]

The UK Defence & Security Export Statistics for 2015[31] state: the "UK share of the global defence export market was estimated at 12 per cent, enabling the UK to maintain its position as one of the most successful defence exporters."

Five of the world's six largest arms sellers are the five Permanent Members of the UN Security Council. This explains why efforts to curb the arms trade have so far failed. I repeat that sentence: this explains why efforts to curb the arms trade have so far failed. It is known as "a seat at the table" — a seat desperately prized by the UK as a badge of still being a great power.

President Obama, Nobel Peace laureate, has allowed sales of one hundred billion dollars' worth of arms to Saudi Arabia. Longstanding US and UK support for Saudi Arabia fed the growth of its Wahhabist movements, which are the ideological home of al-Qa'ida and ISIS.

I am stunned by what I report in these last two paragraphs. How have we the British people been dumbed down into accepting a situation where we are proud to be part of a global trade in lethal weapons that kill or maim hundreds of thousands of people every year?

United Nations Security Council

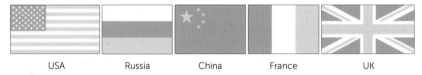

| USA | Russia | China | France | UK |

Top 5 Arms Sellers in 2014

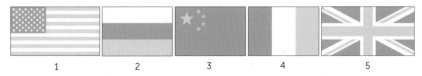

| 1 | 2 | 3 | 4 | 5 |

"Saudi Arabia attacked targets in Yemen using UK-manufactured arms, contributing to a severe humanitarian crisis in the country." According to Amnesty,[32] the attacks amount to war crimes.[33] Saudi Arabia's intervention illustrates how the arms market, including the UK's participation in it, facilitates atrocities and profoundly undermines security across the world, but the British government's security strategy salutes the UK arms industry for its "major part in addressing the threats we face". It says that the UK's "responsible defence and security exports", including sales that it has approved to Saudi Arabia, Bahrain, Egypt, Israel, and other rights-abusing states, are "essential for our security and prosperity".[34]

Britain is now the second biggest arms dealer in the world,[35] since 2010 having sold arms to 22 of the 30 countries on the UK Government's own human rights watch list. A full two-thirds of UK weapons over this period were sold to Middle Eastern countries, where instability has fed into increased risk of terror threats to Britain and across the West.[36]

The British arms trade is protected by government secrecy on contracts and the level of subsidy provided through export credit guarantees and financing of R&D. Whenever the public or Parliament raise criticism, the instant defence is that British jobs are at stake, an assertion that is questionable, as we shall see.

The New York Times described in 2015 how the sale of US arms fuels the wars of Arab states: "To wage war in Yemen, Saudi Arabia is using F-15 fighter jets bought from Boeing. Pilots from United Arab Emirates are flying Lockheed Martin's F-16 to bomb both Yemen and Syria... As the Middle East descends into proxy wars, sectarian conflicts and battles against terrorist networks, countries in the region that have stockpiled American military hardware are now actually using it and wanting more. The result is a boom for American defence contractors ... but also the prospect of a dangerous new arms race in a region where the map of alliances has been sharply re-drawn."[37]

"Some powerful people make their living with the production of arms and sell them to one country for them to use against another country... It's the industry of death, the greed that harms us all, the desire to have more money."[38] — Pope Francis

The Sunni Shia divide in Islam

Sunni and Shia Muslims have lived peacefully together for centuries; in many countries it being common for members of the two sects to intermarry and pray at the same mosques. They share faith in the Quran although differ in doctrine, ritual, law, theology and religious organisation. Shia identity is however said to be rooted in victimhood over the killing of Husayn, the Prophet Mohammed's grandson, in the seventh century, and a long history of marginalisation by the Sunni majority, Islam's dominant sect. Sunni identity, which roughly 85 per cent of the world's 1.6 billion Muslims follow, has viewed Shia Islam with suspicion, and extremist Sunnis have portrayed Shias as heretics and apostates. Many Sunni even say that Shias are not Muslims.

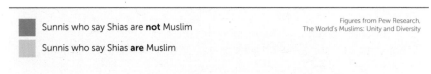

Sunnis who say Shias are **not** Muslim

Sunnis who say Shias **are** Muslim

Figures from Pew Research,
The World's Muslims: Unity and Diversity

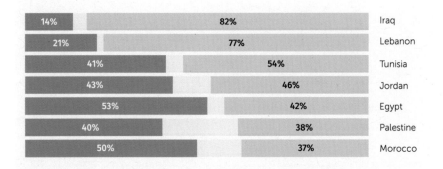

14%	82%	Iraq
21%	77%	Lebanon
41%	54%	Tunisia
43%	46%	Jordan
53%	42%	Egypt
40%	38%	Palestine
50%	37%	Morocco

Recent struggles between Sunni and Shia forces have fed the Syrian civil war that threatens to transform the map of the Middle East, spurred violence that is fracturing Iraq, widened fissures in a number of tense

Gulf countries and sparked a revival of transnational jihadi networks now posing a threat beyond the region.

Two countries that compete for the leadership of Islam, Sunni Saudi Arabia and Shia Iran, have used the sectarian divide to further their ambitions. How their rivalry is settled will likely shape the political balance between Sunnis and Shias and the future of the region, especially in Syria, Iraq, Lebanon, Bahrain, and Yemen. Enmeshed in the proxy battle are the armed militants, motivated by the goals of cleansing the faith or preparing the way for the return of the messiah.[39]

If it bleeds, it leads

The narrative of war intrudes relentlessly into our lives from different sectors of the media. A primary driver of the current media narrative is that war is inevitable, and that violence must be met with violence. This 'shock-horror' approach feeds the public feeling of helplessness and subsequent apathy. Displays of weaponry are glamorised, news media acting as a sales force for arms manufacturers; indeed one of the marketing advantages for a new missile is to be able to put the banner "battle proven" across the photo in the sales brochure. The bombing of Baghdad in March 2003 — known as 'Shock and Awe' — was presented with breathless excitement, like a massive terminator firework display. There was no thought or mention of the human beings burning to death as we watched all those buildings exploding.

Many viewers feel so sick with the endless diet of horror and fear that they no longer watch the news. While there is no question that we need to be informed about conflict in other parts of the world, the way it is done provokes not only anxiety but hopelessness. The effect on younger people especially is alarming, producing numbness, depression and self harm.

The British media prides itself on 'balance' in its reporting, but it does not balance stories of terror with stories of those who prevent or reduce terror. The cultivation of peace is not something we are educated in. The BBC rarely carries a feature on the heroism of those who mediate between warlords, rescue child soldiers, dig old people out of the rubble of bombed buildings, or intervene to stop war.

Decisions on war & strategy are made by those sharing similar values, and the belief that security is achieved through dominance

The UK House of Commons Defence Committee's pronouncements "illustrate the prevailing security narrative, in which the UK and its allies form an island of order in a sea of growing threats, which can only be defeated by coercive instruments of power. This narrative enjoys a general consensus across the defence establishment, defined broadly as central government, the departments of Whitehall, senior officers of the armed forces, strategic studies departments, military think-tanks, arms companies, defence correspondents and commentators. The political power of the establishment ensures that this narrative continues to dominate the policymaking conversation."[40]

A lot of my working life has been spent dealing with British, Chinese and US military establishments, with generals and admirals and senior officials and politicians, and they do consistently assume that they know what is right. This is the assumption on which they establish their power. Issues of defence and security are made out to be too complex for ordinary people to decide on. And if we acquiesce, if we don't take a stand for what we know and believe, then they do have the power because we hand it to them. My experience is that every one I talked with turned out to be a very human being, with the difficult life problems that we all have, although some were more open to dialogue than others.

The defence establishment, which dominates the security discourse, is composed almost entirely of privately-educated men. The Royal United Services Institute's landmark audit of recent British wars, *Wars in Peace: British Military Operations Since 1991*, published in 2014, contains 12 chapters and a foreword, all contributed by men. It was launched by an all-male panel to an audience consisting mostly of men; only one woman spoke during the 90-minute event to ask the only question that dissented significantly from the panel. The leadership of the armed forces and arms industry is also predominantly privately educated men, as are most defence correspondents, commentators and analysts.[41]

Participation in the security policy discourse therefore appears to be restricted to — and restricted by — privileged men who champion the view that military power and alliances of strategic dominance will deliver security and status.

Meanwhile, the voices of those who suffer so brutally in war are not being heard at the peace table, nor are their needs taken into account in peace agreements. A UNIFEM study in 2009 found that women make up only 2.5 per cent of signatories to peace agreements. A review of 31 major peace processes showed that only 4 per cent of participants were women, and that women made up only 2.4 per cent of chief mediators, 3.7 per cent of witnesses, and 9 per cent of negotiators.[42]

The International Crisis Group, globally respected for its incisive and sharply focused reports, said in 2006 that peace-building cannot succeed if half the population is excluded from the process. Crisis Group's research in Sudan, Congo (DRC) and Uganda suggests that peace agreements, post-conflict reconstruction, and governance do better when women are involved.[43] A peace agreement is 35 per cent more likely to last at least 15 years if women participate in its creation.[44]

Inclusive Security reported on the situation in Colombia in December 2016 that: "As late as 2012, zero women were present at the peace negotiating table. Our Network members and others organised; 10,000 people filled the streets in protest. Shortly thereafter, women's representation was increased to nearly one-third."[45]

The other key driver of the arms race is of course competition. As General Houghton, Chief of the UK Defence Staff, put it in 2015: "We are in a state of permanent engagement in a global competition". What competition? The current British national security strategy repeats the declaration of its predecessors in 2010 and 2008, as well as the 1998 Strategic Defence Review, that there is "currently no immediate direct military threat to the UK mainland".[46]

Governments are not truthful to their people about why they go to war, and what's happening during war

On 6 July 2016 Sir John Chilcot reported on a British public inquiry into the nation's role in the Iraq War. The Chilcot Report showed that:

- Saddam Hussein did not pose an urgent threat to British interests
- Intelligence regarding weapons of mass destruction was presented with unwarranted certainty
- Peaceful alternatives to war had not been exhausted
- The UK and the US undermined the authority of the United Nations Security Council
- A war in 2003 was unnecessary.[47]

In December 2002, I was contacted by the former first lady of Greece, Margarita Papandreou, to help lead a delegation of female leaders of the Middle East to find out if there was any way to avoid war in Iraq. After a long struggle to get visas and an equal struggle to actually get to Baghdad, our delegation finally arrived on 3 January, 2003. We met with Iraqi cabinet ministers including Deputy Prime Minister Tariq Aziz, Foreign Minister Nagi Sabri, and Oil Minister Amer Mohammed Rashid, as well as with doctors, teachers, and scientists. We visited sites recently inspected for weapons of mass destruction. After seven days we had collected enough positive information to condense it into a two-page Plan to Tony Blair, outlining in ten points how war could be avoided. It was placed in Blair's hands a few days later. I heard that he read it quickly and said, "It's too late." For Blair, it was. Two months later we discovered that irreversible machinery for the US/UK invasion had been set in motion the previous October and that Blair had given Bush his unconditional support a year previously.[48]

In 2010 WikiLeaks released vast numbers of documents related to the wars in Iraq and Afghanistan revealing that "…US executive war-making is marked by massive deception of the American people — particularly lying about the enormous civilian casualties the US is causing"[49] …

Subsequent Times and Guardian stories describe how these official US documents reveal constant US Executive Branch misleading the American people.

The 'war on terror' — an abject failure — continues unquestioned by governments

"Largely at the behest of the British prime minister, NATO bombed Libya in 2011. Regime change was again a main objective of intervention; once achieved, Libya was left with no functional government or assistance for recovery. This contravened the Security Council mandate, which authorised the use of force to protect civilians, but not to change the government or to support rebel forces. Parts of the country are now an ISIS stronghold."[50]

"The US-led invasion of Iraq in 2003 destroyed its government and economy, precipitating a humanitarian crisis and creating a large population of newly unemployed Sunni men, who were disenfranchised by their new Shia-dominated government. These conditions enabled first al-Qa'ida and then ISIS to grow. Jihadi groups in Syria have been shipped arms by British allies Turkey and Saudi Arabia, among others,[51] while Iran and Russia have done the same for the Syrian government. The UK's notional allies on the ground, the Free Syrian Army, have been selling their US-supplied arms to ISIS, according to Jürgen Todenhöfer who has spent time with some of the militants."[52]

Of the 66 British MPs who spoke in favour of the motion to bomb Syria, "40 said nothing about whether the action would benefit Syrians; of the 26 who did, only four made this their main or joint-main argument for the motion. MPs were much more likely to argue for bombing on the grounds that the UK's Western allies wanted it; 46 proponents of the motion made this argument, of whom 12 made it their main or joint-main argument."[53]

War is often seen as unavoidable in determining outcomes when one group is dissatisfied with what seems achievable by other means and concludes that they can improve the situation for themselves through fighting.

This is not to give the impression that "there is a small minority of powerful men who are destroying the planet" and that "the majority of innocents need to rise up and challenge this behavior". While I can detect elements of this belief within myself, I know it can obscure the important realisation that such people are simply displaying characteristics that we all share in some form. Moreover, we are typically most critical of those characteristics that we have not owned up to, and examined. Hence the need to understand the human side of violent conflict — the rage, greed, fear and lust for power that drive war, whether on a massive scale, or in families. We return to this issue in the final chapter.

People love to fight

Some fundamentalists say that God wants them to fight, or that God wants Armageddon. Others would say it's because they have had an upbringing that gets a buzz out of conflict, or that they suffered so much violence that they had to learn to fight. Yet others would say that a sense of injustice is one of the most powerful motivations for violence, and that the use of any other means will leave them out-manouvred. Others would say, too much testosterone.

A male colleague who has devoted his life to conflict analysis says: "I believe that there are many reasons why violence is appealing. It can be expression of energy, or vitality and exhilaration. It can bring purpose and meaning to a situation where otherwise it is lacking. Other worries become irrelevant when you're focused on survival and winning — it's very simple and zero sum. It can feel heroic, carnal, a move back to some roots or essence. It can involve honour and protection of others. This thing about fighting to right wrongs is heavily infused in our culture and identity. I would argue that 100 per cent of the population is subject to these reasons, and that those not aware of this possibility are largely suppressing it."

It would be good to know just what percentage of the population of the world is "subject to these reasons", or indeed other compulsions to fight. My guess would be about 20 per cent. Let me know what yours is. Even if the percentage is greater, we now not only witness the suffering of the victims of war and are sickened by it, but we also know how to prevent it, so we can certainly find methodical ways to make war obsolete.

Interestingly, Sebastian Unger's research shows the positive effects of war on mental health, citing the great sociologist Emile Durkheim who found that when European countries went to war, suicide rates dropped. "Psychiatric wards in Paris were strangely empty during both world wars, and that remained true even as the German army rolled into the city in 1940. Researchers documented a similar phenomenon during civil wars in Spain, Algeria, Lebanon, and Northern Ireland."[54]

A hardware approach

Over decades, in the words of the Ammerdown Report, western defence and security policies "have been predicated on heavy military spending, the failure to abolish nuclear weapons, pragmatic alliances with despotic governments, the arms trade, arms-racing, multiple coercive interventions in other countries, and torture. Even presuming benign intentions, the securitised enforcement of the prevailing order has ruptured millions of lives, plundered resources, and crippled local and national economies in the process."[55]

This way of thinking relies on a 'hardware' approach: we compete to have the most advanced technological weapons, we send out spies to discover enemy inventions, we build security 'domes' in the sky.

Armed conflict has an extremely high economic cost: violence destroys infrastructure, forces shops and banks to close, and scares investors away from potential and existing markets.

A software approach

We human beings are quite capable of adopting instead a 'software' approach, even at the very top. Software means dealing with people, developing trust, finding common ground. It is what the best of tough leaders do; it's what Mandela did when he came out of prison, in opening dialogue with the white government of South Africa.

He could easily have accepted the vast amounts of armaments being offered to the African National Congress. But he opted for more challenging work, requiring patience, flexibility and wisdom. By using such means he and his colleagues avoided a civil war, which observers predicted would have cost millions of lives.

To conclude this section, a note from His Holiness the Dalai Lama:

"Of course, war and the large military establishments are the greatest sources of violence in the world. Whether their purpose is defensive or offensive, these vast powerful organisations exist solely to kill human beings. We should think carefully about the reality of war. Most of us have been conditioned to regard military combat as exciting and glamorous — an opportunity for men to prove their competence and courage. Since armies are legal, we feel that war is acceptable; in general, nobody feels that war is criminal or that accepting it is criminal attitude. In fact, we have been brainwashed. War is neither glamorous nor attractive. It is monstrous. Its very nature is one of tragedy and suffering."[56]

For at least three thousand years, those making decisions on armaments and war have been schooled in the notion that it is heroic to fight, and that men have a duty to defend their families and territory using whatever force is necessary.

Two major changes have taken place during the last seventy years that must change those assumptions. The first is the development of weapons of such destructive power that their use would terminate human and other life on the planet. The second is that half of the human race that has had little say in decision-making is now slowly finding its voice, its place in public life, and taking a stand on better methods of preventing and resolving conflict.

PART TWO: HOW CAN WAR BE STOPPED?

Chapter 3

The Basic Principles — Dialogue, Prevention and Early Intervention

"If you want peace, don't talk to your friends.
Talk to your enemies." — Desmond Tutu

Preventing war, because it is such an unfamiliar concept to us, requires a substantial shift in assumptions and mind-set. Traditionally it has been assumed that weaponry and 'defence' will bring security, and therefore that more weaponry will bring more security.

However, humanity has now entered a new era where these assumptions require an overhaul.

The major threats to our security now emanate from issues that cannot be dealt with by weaponry: namely global warming, migration, the rich-poor gap, and cyber attack. Our security now depends on our ability to co-operate with nations who might previously have been our enemies, and our ability to use the skills and knowledge gained in the past century that enable us to avoid the catastrophic consequences of recent wars. These include three basic principles: dialogue, prevention and early intervention.

Dialogue

Attempts to stop war from the top down often fail because of the mind-sets — fear, aggression, competition, greed — qualities shared by most of those leaders filtered to the top by our current systems. One of the best ways to overcome the force of these attitudes and emotions is by systematically building trust through dialogue.

The Oxford Process is a tried and tested programme developed by Oxford Research Group over three decades. It builds on a track record of facilitating a unique type of discreet high-level dialogue between the parties to some of the world's most intractable conflicts. It uses the tools of geo-political insight and analysis, cultural savvy and human psychology to understand and manage both the tensions and the human relationships that underpin conflict.

Today Gabrielle Rifkind directs the Oxford Process programme, concentrating on preventive diplomacy work and high-level mediation. Her experience, like mine, is that behind the aggressive façade of negotiations are human beings. Some are not telling the truth, some have ordered or undertaken brutal acts, and all are under immense pressure from the constituencies behind them.

Gabrielle has facilitated a number of Track II roundtables in the Middle East on the Israel-Palestine conflict, as well as on the conflict over Iran's nuclear programme. Committed to trying to understand the mind-set of the region, she has facilitated meetings with and spent time talking to the leadership in Syria, Iran, Lebanon, Egypt, Jordan, Saudi Arabia, Israel, and 'western' states.

The experience gained elsewhere — in Northern Ireland and Colombia for example — can now be put to much more extensive use to prevent future conflicts escalating into war. Individuals such as Jonathan Powell, Senator George Mitchell, Mary Robinson, Hina Jilani and Martti Ahtisaari can all give helpful guidance on how to prevent war, and could train others in their invaluable skills.

If the aim is to stop the cycle of violence, it is imperative to develop skills to change the dialogue. The most essential of these skills is to insist on mutual listening, not only to the words being said, but to the feelings behind them. This shows respect, and as we saw in the opening story, respect is the most powerful antidote to humiliation. Humiliation is one, if not the, strongest driver of violence. "Getting into the mind of the enemy can often be far more persuasive than the most fearsome weapons."[57]

When I started the Oxford Research Group in 1982, I was driven by fear — fear of nuclear holocaust, and anger that the world's population was being exposed to the possibility not only of poisoning from unsafe — guarded nuclear materials, but of global nuclear holocaust caused either by lunatic decisions, or by accident.

In 1983 this very nearly happened: for a few crucial moments on 26 September, 1983, Stanislav Petrov held the fate of the world in his hands. When an alarm suddenly went off at Soviet nuclear early warning centre Serpukhov-15, Stanislav was responsible for reacting to a report that five American nuclear missiles were heading toward the Soviet Union. Rather than inform his superiors, who he knew would decide to retaliate, Stanislav followed his gut feeling and went against protocol, convincing the armed forces that it was a false alarm. His decision saved the world from a potentially devastating nuclear holocaust.[58]

It took me some years to discover that if we wanted to communicate with those who had power over nuclear decisions, it was vital to realise that they also — albeit for different reasons — were driven by fear. By 1988 we had published our fourth book, entitled "The Nuclear Weapons World — Who, Where and How", which contained the biographies of 650 nuclear weapons decision-makers in Britain, France, China, the USA and the [then] Soviet Union.

In research for my doctorate I interviewed 13 of these decision-makers, including generals, the most senior officials in ministries of defence, physicists who designed warheads, defence contractors, people who signed the cheques, and the politicians (who eventually announced decisions that had been made many years previously, without any democratic debate). After listening to each of them for several hours, I drew cognitive maps of how they thought. What I discovered was that in 12 out of 13 cases the 'sink' — namely the basic assumption on which all their thought patterns were based — was 'the threat'. So these men were all driven by a sense of being under threat.

I asked if they would like to see the cognitive maps I had made, and each person agreed. This allowed us to understand each other's thought processes, and speaking to them straightforwardly helped to develop trust. With some trust established, it was possible to invite them or their colleagues to spend two days in a medieval manor house near Oxford to talk with their most knowledgeable critics on key issues of nuclear weapons policy. For example, we would bring together a leading warhead designer from Los Alamos in the US with a physicist who had quit his senior post at Aldermaston (the UK warhead design centre) to become director of an internationally respected peace research institute in Stockholm.

The subject under discussion might, for example, be control of fissile materials, or a No First Use policy — a pledge that a country would not use nuclear weapons unless it had been attacked with nuclear weapons. After the initial suspicion and mistrust had subsided, due to the way all participants were treated and how the meetings were facilitated, participants were rolling up their sleeves and thrashing out possible terms for treaties.

It took about fifteen years to get to this point. One key ingredient was complete confidentiality — there were no press releases, no communiqués, and nothing of these meetings was ever reported in the media. Building trust between participants was essential. The same is true of the nuclear dialogues conducted by the Oxford Research Group today.

The British government knows, from our experience in Northern Ireland, that what finally brought 30 years of terror to an end was not the application of superior force. It was the building of bridges, listening, patient mediation, respect and dialogue. Senator George Mitchell, who played a major part in the eventual Good Friday Agreement, said: "I will listen for as long as it takes."[59]

No lasting peace without trust

Communication, trauma counselling and bridge building may not appear to be very glamorous skills. But peace workers depend on these skills every single day, as the bedrock of their work. This is because no peace agreement, however painstakingly negotiated, will hold for long without trust being built.

Trust gets shattered in war. But trust is also being eroded in apparently peaceful societies. When politicians make claims that they subsequently by-pass or ignore, as in the Brexit campaigns, the electorate turns sour. When church hierarchies cover up the sexual abuse of children by priests, people lose faith. When media outlets fan the flames of fake news, readers drown in a tsunami of falsehood. When banks, who are supposed to take care of our money, open accounts in customers' names without their consent, we get scared.

So now we have to examine not what leaders say, but what they do. Traditionally we may have assumed that the ethics of a country came from the top down. Now it has to come from the bottom up. That means we the people need to inspect our own truth record. I need to ask myself: "What are my own red lines that I would not cross? When do I exaggerate for impact? What beliefs of mine do I know I can trust?"

Trust is a source of power. This is because integrity has an energy all its own. People can detect it, feel it, smell it. You know what it feels like when someone gives you their word, and you can sense if you can trust that word. It is that trust that is the foundation of security. It makes us safe. If we want a safer world, it starts here.

Prevention

A co-ordinated strategy for peace will concentrate on the prevention of armed conflict, co-ordinated with dialogue and early intervention. This joined up strategy is necessary because "we look at those who take the big political decisions on war, and we see the gulf that separates them from the civilians who have to face the consequences."[60] The overall strategy is to develop a whole systems approach to the building of peace worldwide, from the local level, to national, regional and global levels.

The keys to successful prevention of war are respect, speed of reaction and developing an understanding of how power works. All the research I have seen over 35 years shows me that the main cause of fighting is humiliation. And the best antidote to humiliation is respect, as demonstrated by US Lieutenant Colonel Chris Hughes in the opening story. Military officers are beginning to realise the contribution they could

A Liberian Nobel Peace Laureate says: "In Liberia right now, there are hundreds of thousands of unemployed young people, and they're ready-made mercenaries for wars in West Africa. You'd think the international community would be sensible enough to know they should work to change this. But they aren't."[61]

make to preventing armed conflict. Senior military officers from the UK and six other countries collaborated to produce a major report in 2014, *Understand to Prevent (U2P)*, which seeks to effect "a shift of military effort from crisis response (waiting for the future to happen) to 'upstream' engagement to positively manage conflict, prevent violence and build peace."[62] The report concludes that "military involvement is only ever in support of wider efforts to counter violent conflict. We have embraced the comprehensive approach throughout but have identified that, in the upstream prevention period, coordination between the comprehensive players — diplomatic, economic, military, non-government organisations, civil society and business — does not exist. The U2P concept therefore proposes establishing forums to bring together various stakeholders to help a host nation with a 'prevent' task. We call this a comprehensive contact team."

There will be more about these potentially excellent plans in a later section on multi-stakeholder dialogue. A further incentive to develop prevention of armed conflict lies in the disastrous effects of military action on global warming. The Pentagon, for example, is the single largest institutional user of petroleum products and energy in the world.[63] Yet the Pentagon has a blanket exemption in all international climate agreements.

Early intervention

To be effective prevention has to happen swiftly once tensions become apparent. For external action to be taken in a conflict situation involves the national interests of countries concerned, and therefore calculations about the investment of capacity, popular support and political will. Rarely are all three in place at the same time in one country.

With no early-warning system in place, the result can be an entire lack of action resulting in genocide, as in the Rwandan case. Or it can mean delays and inconsistency resulting in a local conflict exploding to involve ancient regional fissures, as in Syria, with fanatical elements converging on a chaotic situation. This has caused the deaths of over 400,000 people, the displacement of over 12 million — half the country — and the emergence of violent, extremist groups like ISIS.

According to the International Institute for Strategic Studies there are around 75 places in the world where tensions could break out into war at any given time.

Leymah Gbowee led a women's peace movement that helped bring an end to the Second Liberian Civil War in 2003, using efficient grassroots early warning systems. Such early warning, whether by grassroots intelligence or by complex radar systems, is clearly vital to the prevention of armed conflict. *The Armed Conflict Location & Event Data Project* and *The Early Warning Project* — described more fully in the next chapter — provide regular analysis of at-risk countries and evolving situations.

Possibly the most important overall aspect of prevention concerns an understanding of power. Most of us understand power as hierarchy, authority, rule, physical strength and ultimately military force. It emanates from outside a person — from armies or weapons or wealth or constituencies or status or god. It is essentially a question of having power over something or somebody else. This kind of power may be called 'domination power'.

However there is another kind of power, essentially a question of power with others. It co-operates rather than competes. It's creative, and has an extraordinary energy, because it comes from within a person. Thus it depends on no-one and nothing other than the integrity and authority of an individual. This may be invisible to the objective eye but immediately obvious to the senses. It is also available in the instant, and can thus hold the balance between life and death. It is sometimes called 'inner power', of which we shall see some remarkable examples in the next chapter.

"Everything now depends on man: immense power of destruction is given into his hand and the question is whether he can resist the will to use it, and can temper his will with the spirit of love and wisdom."[64] — C.G. Jung

Chapter 4

The Basic Strategy for Building Peace: How it Works

Those experienced in worldwide initiatives to prevent war tend to prioritise building peace 'from the bottom up'. Thus the strategy starts with the methods found to be most effective at local levels, followed by what can best be done by national governments, concluding with the systems that work best at a global level.

In each case I shall briefly outline the principle (the concept and its desired outcomes), followed by an example of how this works in practice, followed by the plan of how the principle can now be implemented. These plans will be costed in the next chapter.

Systems that effectively prevent conflict and build safety at local levels

1. The value of locally-led peace-building

PRINCIPLE

Local people know best how to prevent armed violence. 'Locally-led' initiatives are now recognised as effective and cost effective. In 2006 the UK Department for International Development (DfID) produced an economic rationale for its strategic peace-building focus, reporting that on average the annual cost of one violent conflict is equal to all global development aid in a year.[65]

Locally-led civilian initiatives to prevent killing are now widespread in conflict areas, and have been recognised and supported by organisations like Responding to Conflict (RTC) who produced four case studies of local peace-building back in 2000.

In 2001 the Oxford Research Group was able to identify 350 civilian peace-building initiatives worldwide, of which it reported on 50 of the most effective.[66] As a result the organisation Peace Direct was set up, to support grassroots peace-builders, because local people tend to know best how to resolve local conflicts. Peace Direct's research in turn resulted in Insight on Conflict, an initiative that has now become a leading online resource on local peace-building in conflict zones worldwide and currently reports on over 1,410 peace-building organisations across 44 different conflict-affected regions.[67]

Organisations such as Conciliation Resources,[68] International Alert[69] Global Action to Prevent War,[70] and Search for Common Ground[71] are working with thousands of local peace builders to ensure their hard-earned skills can permeate upwards all over the world. These skills include strengthening the rule of law, reconciliation between clans, exchanging bicycles and sewing machines for weapons, bridge building, setting up alert networks, mediation, consultation with religious leaders, setting up truth & reconciliation commissions, training mediators, freeing child soldiers, violence reduction education in schools, and leadership training for women.

EXAMPLE

Gulalai Ismael lives in NW Pakistan, one of the most dangerous places in the world to be a woman. Aged 15 she started an organisation called Aware Girls to enable females to go to school. Malala Yousefzai was shot in the head for doing just this. Gulalai has now trained 20 teams of young men and women in Pakistan and Afghanistan to prevent other young people joining extremist groups and to promote a culture of non violence. Using the tools of listening and dialogue, they have reached and dissuaded more than 500 teenagers 'at risk' of becoming extremist.[72]

PLAN

Funding to be made available to at least 1,400 effective locally led peace-building organisations across 44 different conflict-affected regions, for a period of 10 years.

. . . .

The irony is, that while soldiers are rightly awarded medals for bravery, there are few if any awards for the type of extraordinary courage demanded daily by work like that of Gulalai and so many like her. They need encouragement — letters of support — and media coverage to make them safer.

If you know media writers/presenters, alert them to the stories constantly appearing on https://www.peacedirect.org

2. Active regional platforms for a joined-up approach

PRINCIPLE

To be systematically effective, locally-led peace-builders' initiatives must receive reliable funding. Generally they do not, largely because major donors took to saying that funding 'small' initiatives is 'messy'. This is no longer true. The prevention approach is ready to be built into an active platform for local peace-building, which will require dedicated funding. Thus continuous local systems analysis will unite smaller civil-society elements into a network, pooling knowledge and promoting a 'joined-up' approach. The platform will demonstrate to donors and crowd funders the use of transparent and effective mechanisms for deciding priorities and evaluating the most effective organisations to carry them out, as well as for monitoring their impact.

EXAMPLE

Sweden is ahead of the game. On 27 May, 2016 the Stockholm International Peace Research Institute (SIPRI) released the fifth film in its series, titled *A Year of Reflection on Peace and Security: Peace-building in Mali and why supporting civil society matters.* The film features Swedish Foreign Minister Margot Wallström and UN Deputy Secretary General Jan Eliasson discussing SIPRI's ongoing support to Malian civil society's peace-building efforts.[73]

3. Breaking the cycle of violence through training, consultation and bridge building

PRINCIPLE

Break the cycle of violence at an early stage. The cycle of violence starts with the political response to a perceived threat, followed by demonising an 'enemy', and the call to action and aggression. Atrocities cause terror and trauma, followed by grief and then anger. If nothing is done at this stage, anger leads to the drive for retaliation and revenge, causing an escalation of atrocities.[75] Thus the cycle of violence is perpetuated over generations and even centuries.

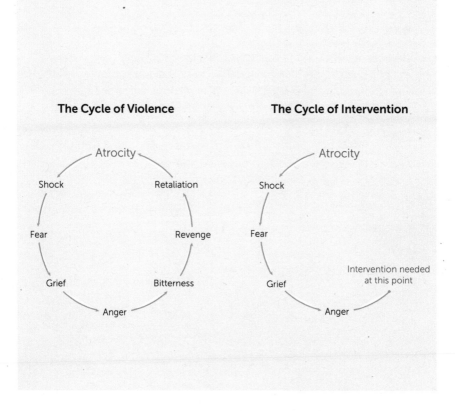

The Cycle of Violence

Atrocity
Shock   Retaliation
Fear   Revenge
Grief   Bitterness
      Anger

The Cycle of Intervention

Atrocity
Shock
Fear
                Intervention needed
                at this point
Grief
      Anger

The cycle can be broken by providing physical, political and psychological security through tried and tested methods of conflict prevention.[76] Therefore the Business Plan involves training women, consultation with religious leaders, bridge building, setting up truth & reconciliation commissions, training mediators, freeing child soldiers, trauma counselling and strengthening the rule of law.

EXAMPLE

It is estimated that 250,000 children are fighting in wars all over the world. In DR Congo, former child soldiers are penetrating deep into the bush to liberate children who have been kidnapped by militias. They do this by negotiating with the militias to exchange one goat (price $5) for one child, and they bring the children home. Then begins the challenging work of re-integrating deeply traumatised children into their communities.[77]

PLAN

Break the cycle of violence by encouraging new local systems to provide physical, political and psychological security through tried and tested methods of conflict prevention. This can be carried out by existing peace and conflict resolution organisations with appropriate support.

. . . .

4. Addressing the persistent and long-term influence and effects of trauma

PRINCIPLE

When people have suffered massive loss and trauma, the memory of this can remain in the collective psyche for generations. Therefore it is imperative to recognise, respect and acknowledge the wrong that was done, and the atrocities inflicted, even many centuries ago. The answer is trauma counselling, through which ancient wounds can be healed and the pattern of revenge relinquished.

EXAMPLE

Jo Berry is the daughter of Sir Anthony Berry, a British conservative politician killed in the 1984 Brighton bombing. Jo has not only reconciled with the Brighton Bomber, the man who killed her father, but now works with him to build peace in Northern Ireland.[78]

PLAN

Widespread training schemes to be set up to share knowledge of how trauma counselling works, and to adapt and develop practices suited to different cultures. This can be carried out by trauma counselling organisations — such as the International Association of Trauma Professionals[79] — setting up 'out-reach training' in appropriate languages.

....

Systems that effectively prevent conflict and build safety at national/regional levels

5. National Infrastructures for Peace

PRINCIPLE

An Infrastructure for Peace, pioneered in South Africa by Nelson Mandela, develops Peace Councils at national, regional, city, town and even village levels through which all relevant stakeholders can co-operate in systematically building peace and preventing violent conflict.[80] If there is no national strategy to contain violence, it can quickly develop into civil war. Therefore the Infrastructure recruits respected community leaders to join the Councils where they are trained in violence prevention methods and required to develop a Peace Plan for their area, should violence break out.

EXAMPLE

One of the first countries to establish an Infrastructure for Peace was South Africa, where leaders realised the risk of civil war after Mandela was released and before negotiations could lead to elections. Now the governments of Ghana and Kenya are pioneering the implementation of their own Infrastructures for Peace. Both countries had general elections recently and these structures (even in embryo) helped in preventing and reducing post-election violence. The costs are small; for example the first three years of setting up an Infrastructure for Peace in Ghana cost some $2.5 million and was paid by UNDP. Other countries such as Costa Rica now have a Ministry of Peace.[81]

PLAN

Ten governments to build national Infrastructures for Peace.

....

6. Enable qualified women to fill policy-making roles on peace & security

PRINCIPLE

Women are shown to be the most effective and tenacious peacebuilders. However more than 90 per cent of negotiators and those in policy-making positions on peace and conflict are male, meaning that the suffering and trauma of women and children in war are not taken into account at the peace table.

Ambassador Swanee Hunt and the 'Women Waging Peace Policy Commission' have conducted 15 field-based case studies to document women's contributions to conflict prevention, peace negotiations, and post-war reconstruction. This has yielded a network of more than 1,000 trained women leaders from more than 30 conflicts. Their partnership with key international women's organisations — UNIFEM, Global Fund for Women, International Alert's Gender and Peacebuilding Programme — and contact with women's organisations in 20 conflict countries, would add to lists of suitably qualified women and develop strategies to ensure their acceptance in policy-making positions and peace negotiations.

EXAMPLE

None of the five tribes represented at the Somali peace talks in 1999 would allow a single woman on their delegation. So Asha Hagi Elmi, a respected female leader, formed her own delegation consisting only of women. This resulted in 12 per cent of seats in the new parliament being reserved for women, and now there are 4 female government ministers — even more remarkable in a conservative Islamist state.

PLAN

Enable qualified women to fill policy-making roles on peace and security. This will need research, in order to present profiles of suitably qualified women in 30 conflict affected countries to relevant authorities and lobby for their acceptance in policy-making roles and negotiations. This programme could be supervised by Inclusive Security who strengthen women leaders through targeted training and mentoring, helping them to build coalitions, and connecting them to policymakers.[82]

Asha Hagi Elmi

7. Women successfully counter extremism

PRINCIPLE

Recent examples demonstrate how women in areas of violent extremism have become the most effective antidote to terror (note that this is 'on the ground' work, in contrast to the above example where women are being trained for policy-making positions). "In every setting, women's rights groups have been the first to notice and often bear the brunt of these regressive forces. They have been warning against the rise of extremist forces across the Americas, Asia, Africa and the Middle East for nearly three decades.

...local women-led NGOs and community based organisations working in Iraq, Syria, Pakistan, and elsewhere have developed innovative approaches to tackle the spreading ideologies and practices of extreme state and non-state actors directly affecting their communities.

...The reality on the ground across countries affected by extremism is that these pro-peace and pro-plurality women-led organisations and movements that are locally rooted yet transnational have the credibility and authenticity to counter rising extremism and offer an alternative vision of the future in which disaffected men and women can feel a sense of belonging and purpose. The international community would improve its approaches if they drew on the leadership and knowledge of such local actors."[83]

EXAMPLE

War-torn northern Syria may be the most unexpected place to find genuine gender equality. Yet the women's umbrella organisation Kongira Star in Rojava has set up an autonomous, grassroots, democratic structure which has resulted in shifting patriarchal mindsets and reversing gender discriminatory laws. It is an exercise in direct grassroots democracy.

"At the neighbourhood level, they have set up communes ranging in size from 7 to 300 families depending on whether they are based in villages or cities. All the members elect a man and a woman under the co-presidentship rule to manage the work and to represent their interests at the next level, the House of the People — a kind of regional council." [84]

The women have formed brigades to resist the waves of masked jihadis razing towns, fields and cities, wreaking terror. They did what no one else, not Iraq's army, not the Kurds' fabled Peshmerga, nor Western bombs, had managed to achieve. It was they, above all, who engineered the liberation of the Yazidis from Daesh warriors. Now they are improvising a new model of living in an enclave that is not an ethnic state but a confederation of half a dozen ethnicities, organising co-operative economy in an egalitarian borderland called Rojava. [85]

PLAN

Women's organisations in every country or region at risk of violent extremism to receive funding to learn from the methods employed by Kongira Star and other similar initiatives, using films made by such award-winning directors as Deeyah Khan and her film investigating the deeper reason for suicide bombings. [86]

8. Breaking the cycle of violence through Truth and Reconciliation (TRC)

PRINCIPLE

The transparency developed through the TRC process is capable of breaking the cycle of violence. Historic violations of human rights, even including murders, torture and massacres, can be assuaged and even healed by a process of encouragement to perpetrators that telling the truth about their actions can bring about closure and forgiveness.

EXAMPLE

Archbishop Desmond Tutu was the chairman of South Africa's Truth and Reconciliation Commission. The TRC was created by Nelson Mandela's Government of National Unity in 1995 to help South Africans come to terms with their extremely troubled past. It was established to investigate the violations that took place between 1960 and 1994, to provide support and reparation to victims and their families, and to compile a full and objective record of the effects of apartheid on South African society.

Desmond Tutu says that "To forgive is not just to be altruistic. It is the best form of self-interest... However, when I talk of forgiveness I mean the belief that you can come out the other side a better person. A better person than the one being consumed by anger and hatred. Remaining in that state locks you in a state of victimhood, making you almost dependent on the perpetrator. If you can find it in yourself to forgive then you are no longer chained to the perpetrator. You can move on, and you can even help the perpetrator to become a better person too."[87]

PLAN

Truth and Reconciliation Commissions to be set up in 4 regions or countries that have undergone historic or recent extreme violations of human rights, such as Northern Ireland or Colombia, in order to prevent the repetition of the cycle of violence.

9. Re-vamp national budgets for prevention of conflict

PRINCIPLE

Only when funds have been set aside by a government specifically for the prevention of conflict can progress be made as compared to the expense of intervening once armed violence has taken place.

EXAMPLE

In 2015 the UK government set up the Conflict Stability and Security Fund (CSSF) to "support our national security interests through conflict prevention, peace-building, stabilisation, peacekeeping and conflict resolution". For 2016 CSSF funding has increased to £1.127 billion and it will increase by a further 19 per cent over the next spending review period, reaching £1.322 billion a year by 2019. But even so, the peacekeeping and stabilisation budgets continue to have first call on available resources. In 2015 a mere £239 million was allocated to conflict prevention! By contrast the UK Defence Budget for 2014/15 was £36.43 billion — 152 times greater than the conflict-prevention budget.

PLAN

The UN and NATO to set standards for all member nations to establish Conflict Prevention funds with a requirement that these funds amount to a specific per cent of their defence budget, just as NATO guidelines encourage all members to spend 2 per cent of their respective country's GDP on their own military defense. In addition to this citizens can campaign for a law that establishes a ratio between their national defence expense and conflict prevention allocations. I think there is room for this change.

10. Cut government support for arms trading and use these funds to develop strategies for diversification

PRINCIPLE

One way to reduce arms exports is to remove government support and funding. According to official annual reports, support for military deals accounted for 47 per cent of all UK export credits in 2012/13. The UK government also subsidises the arms trade by providing marketing and promotional support, mainly through the UKTI Defence and Security Group. Overall, the industry costs the taxpayer £763m per year, according to Oxford Research Group/Saferworld report: *The Subsidy Trap.*[88]

Public subsidy for jobs related to arms exports is also calculated to be in the region of £700 million per annum by the respected Stockholm International Peace Research Institute (SIPRI). In the words of the Financial Times International Economy Editor, "You can have as many arms export jobs as you are prepared to waste public money subsidising." Hence the need to persuade governments to divest from arms trade and invest instead in socially useful products such as green technology.

EXAMPLE

Probably the most famous diversification project was the Lucas Aerospace Corporate Plan, published by the cross-union combined committee in 1976, which included a detailed section on alternative energy. The document spelt out detailed plans for heat pumps, solar cells and fuel cells, windmills and flexible power packs, as well as a road-rail public transportation vehicle, a new hybrid power pack for motor vehicles and airships. In retrospect it is obvious how innovative and ahead of its time this plan was! Chrysler car workers also developed a similar approach, demanding diversification into public transport and agricultural vehicles.[89]

PLAN

Produce and implement strategies for diversification: the ingenuity of engineers now employed in the arms industry would be redeployed to turn the UK into a world leader in green technology. Campaign Against the Arms Trade has estimated that the transition would provide twice as many science and engineering jobs as arms exports do now.[90]

....

11. Switch investment from arms production to renewable energy

PRINCIPLE

Major corporations and investors are alert to the advantages of divesting from unethical investment, such as arms production, because peaceful environmentally-conscious societies are becoming a gold-mine for new sources of progress and profitability.

Global renewable energy statistics for 2015 were published in June 2016. Jeremy Leggett reports that "... investment in renewables is now twice that going to coal & gas combined." Solar PV (photo-voltaics) global capacity continues to rise exponentially as a consequence. Onshore wind and PV will "win the cost race" globally and become the cheapest two energy options in many nations by 2020. In some markets, they already are. In India, solar has become the fastest-growing new energy source. China is on course to generate fully a quarter of its electricity from wind power by 2030.

EXAMPLES

In February 2016 Norway's huge sovereign wealth fund, the world's biggest, announced it had sold out of 73 companies in the past year because their social or environmental policies could hurt profitability. The Norwegian parliament played a crucial role: back in 2004 it helped develop ethical guidelines for the Norwegian Government Pension Fund

Rose Owino, a tailor in Migori, using a **SolarAid** light to charge her phone.

Global to include divestment from companies involved in production of components for nuclear weapons. Since then, ten such companies have been excluded from its portfolio. Similar initiatives have been effectively pursued by legislators in New Zealand and Switzerland.[91]

Dong was once an oil and gas company: its name stands for Danish Oil and Gas. Now 75 per cent of its capital is going into renewables. Lesson: oil and gas companies can make it across the energy transition, no matter what Shell and the others tell us.[92]

The switch to renewables as profitable economic opportunities now echoes around the globe. In April 2016 the Saudi government announced a $2 trillion investment fund to wean their nation off oil within 20 years. Greening energy supplies with renewable energy initiatives works well — not only for the world but also for company profits.

AT&T is saving $86 million a year in energy costs from roughly 8,700 energy projects launched within the past two years, and Tesco estimates that energy efficiency projects dating back to 2006 are now saving the company $320 million a year.[93] Costa Rica is well on its way to becoming the first developing country to have 100 per cent renewable electricity. In 2015 Costa Rica had 100 per cent renewable power for 94 consecutive days[94]. According to the Guardian, by 2016, 98% of Costa Rica's energy was green. This achievement took several decades to build and the next milestone is to ensure that the electricity system is 100 per cent renewable the whole year.[95]

PLAN

A major campaign to persuade pension and sovereign wealth funds to divest from arms production and into Innovative financing linked to renewable energy, beneficial to individuals and communities. This is breaking out even in the large corporate sector. In June 2016, Marks and Spencer unveiled a scheme to crowdfund customer-owned solar for its stores, offering a 5 per cent rate of return for customers who invest in it. This campaign will need to reach all major investment advisers and parliamentary representatives of countries with sovereign wealth funds, and will be costly. In summer 2017 Blackrock, the largest institutional investor in the world, publicly stated they will question each major oil company as to their strategy on the UN Sustainable Development Goals.

12. Multi-Stakeholder Dialogue

PRINCIPLE

Every two years a Multi-Stakeholder Dialogue needs to take place between the main actors in the peace-building field, to discuss the principle causes of violent conflict and how they can most effectively be addressed. This needs to take place at both national and regional levels. Stakeholders must if possible include not only governments, UN agencies, civil society organisations, the military, academic researchers, civil society and police, but also those who have a vested interest in war — resource speculators, arms traders, people traffickers and currency smugglers.

Such dialogue would enable policy makers to establish, with information from the grassroots, which are the most effective methods to address the main causes of conflict, and to draw up workable budgets accordingly.

EXAMPLE

The *Understand to Prevent* report (previously mentioned) was produced by senior officers from the UK, Australia, Canada, Finland, Netherlands, Norway and the USA — all members of the Multinational Capability Development Campaign. Their report understood that military involvement "is only ever in support of wider efforts to counter violent conflict". The report recommends:

"Establishing forums to bring together various stakeholders to help a host nation with a 'prevent' task. We call this a comprehensive contact team [which] is a facilitating and supporting forum, open to agencies and actors seeking to support the prevention of violent conflict in a specific host nation. They will be able to exchange information and therefore increase their understanding of the conflict. Their approach will be multi-layered and multi-dimensional, hence the need for coordination. Their aim will be to engage local actors to find local solutions to transform the conflict. Developing this contact team model — its composition, methodologies and leadership (if any) — is proposed as the central theme of a subsequent project."[96]

PLAN

Every two years a Multi-Stakeholder Dialogue to take place between the main actors in the peace-building field, to discuss the principle causes of violent conflict and how they can most effectively be addressed.

....

13. Peace Buildings. Note the plural

PRINCIPLE

In countries where there is armed conflict there is a deep need for a building where people can gather to do the following:
- train peace-builders and develop capacity
- develop their strategies for peace
- draft legislation for an Infrastructure for Peace
- form alliances between organisations
- hold press conferences, exhibitions, concerts
- gather research and concentrate information
- build a national peace budget.

So the plan is to engage with governments of countries subject to armed conflict, who would like to be the first to have a central Peace Building. A world-class architect is then commissioned to design an extraordinary, inspiring and functional building that would reflect the culture and traditions of the country. The multi-award-winning British architect Thomas Heatherwick has already expressed interest; his Seed Cathedral, the UK pavilion for the Shanghai World Expo in 2010, won the event's top prize, the gold medal for pavilion design.

EXAMPLE

Germany is already contributing to Africa's peace and security architecture by financing a new building housing the African Union's Peace and Security Department in Addis Ababa. The Federal Foreign Office has allocated approximately 27 million euros to finance the new premises.

German foreign minister Steinmeier has praised Ethiopia as playing a key role in helping to resolve numerous regional conflicts and participating in AU peace missions. Angela Merkel opened the new building on 14 October 2016.

PLAN

To provide the world's 10 most conflict-affected countries — Libya, Sudan, Ukraine, Central African Republic, Yemen, Somalia, Afghanistan, Iraq, South Sudan, Syria — with a Peace Building in each country. This could be funded from the countries at the top of the Global Peace Index, see principle 19 below. Which corporates will sponsor a Peace Building in one of the world's most war-torn countries?

Systems that effectively prevent conflict and build safety at international levels

"History tells us that it is easier to get into a conflict than to get out; war and its consequences have their dangerous algorithms, feeding on themselves with a devastating momentum of their own. The road to war may look like a careful strategic assessment; more likely it is mired in a deep fog of misunderstanding and misreading which can unleash an unpredictable chain of events, with governments going to war with little understanding of the consequences."[97]

14. Set up the United Nations Emergency Peace Service

PRINCIPLE

The time has come to put into practice a permanent UN Emergency Peace Service (UNEPS) — a project already fully planned — to ensure that 'Never Again' will there be genocide or crimes against humanity. Such a permanent service would have prevented many of the atrocities that have killed millions of civilians, wounded millions more, forced tens of millions from their homes, destroyed entire economies, and wasted hundreds of billions of dollars.

EXAMPLE

Dr Peter Langille has outlined the UNEPS as a permanent, integrated UN formation, a highly trained and well-equipped first-responder ready for immediate deployment upon authorisation of the UN Security Council; composed of 16,000 dedicated personnel (recruited professionals, selected, trained and employed by the UN); at sufficient strength to operate in high-threat environments.[98]

Because governments have not created the necessary UN capability for an Emergency Peace Service, the responsibility now lies with civil society, working with allies in the UN and interested governments to spread awareness about the UNEPS Plan, expand its network of supporters and secure agreement on its principles, composition and financing.[99] Depending on its final structure and field operations, start up expenses for UNEPS would amount to $2 billion, with an annual recurring cost of $900 million.[100]

Core elements of the Plan include: UNEPS would be a permanent standing capacity based at UN-designated sites, capable of response to an emergency within 48 hours of authorisation, coherently organised under a unified UN command. It would involve as many as 15,000 personnel, individually recruited from many different countries and demonstrating skills in conflict resolution, humanitarian assistance, law enforcement and other peacekeeping capacities.

PLAN

Civil society organisations to engage with the UN Sustainable Development Goals to support Plan 16 for a global brake on the arms trade, and divert part of the 2.5 per cent tax to fund the UN Emergency Peace Service.

....

15. Regional Mediation

PRINCIPLE

Autonomous independent mediation teams to supplement national diplomacy. An internationally accepted culture of mediation is needed to address deteriorating political situations threatening to break out into armed conflict, whether within the borders of a state or between states. While traditional diplomacy is a key tool there are cases where it is of little effect, because diplomats ultimately represent the interests of their respective states and cannot therefore be seen as credible independent mediators.

"Mediator teams need to retain a degree of autonomy, while being able to respond with speed and agility and not get caught in the quagmire of bureaucracies. To claim any sort of legitimacy the mediators need to be seen as independent. At the same time they need direct lines of communication and to be credible with multinational institutions and the stakeholders concerned. They also need to be able to feed back to governments at the highest levels where decisions are made.

Teams would include nationals of the countries where conflict was brewing, who would be best placed to explain the realities on the ground and the perceptions and attitudes of the countries and stakeholders concerned...

...While early intervention at a local level will be of key importance, what happens at a governmental level will also be critical. And what appears to be a local conflict may be stoked by countries engaging in proxy wars in the region, for example in the funding and training of militias. This underlies the importance of connecting the different levels of mediation."[101]

EXAMPLE

The film *Pray the Devil Back to Hell* chronicles the remarkable story of West African women who came together to end the Liberian civil war. Thousands of women — ordinary mothers, grandmothers, aunts and daughters, both Christian and Muslim — came together to pray for peace and then staged a silent protest outside where militias were supposed to be making a peace agreement. When no progress was made in the talks, the women intervened, ultimately preventing the men leaving until agreement was reached. Their actions were critical in bringing about agreement and ending the war.

PLAN

Five regional mediator teams to be set up, to include representatives of different cultures, ethnicities and belief systems, trained and resourced to become available at short notice. These teams could operate under the auspices of the World Peace Support Organisation, proposed in Plan 2 above.

....

16. Campaign for global brake on arms trading

PRINCIPLE

A 2.5 per cent tax levied on current annual arms sales — $94.5 billion — would yield approximately $2,360,000,000. This revenue would be invested in addressing the root causes of conflict, including the Plans formulated above.

If the fallacious argument that defence jobs are sacrosanct is discredited, the next argument usually put forward is that "if we don't supply, others will". This sad response shows no progress in thinking since the arguments in defence of the slave trade. This plan therefore addresses the ethical response to arms trading, while Plans 10 and 11 address the financial aspects.

The political will for this is obviously key. Ministers have told me that if the public kicks up enough noise on an issue, and the press picks it up, they have to think more seriously about how to respond.

EXAMPLE

The US Global Campaign on Military Spending (GCOMS), for example, has called for a global reduction of 10 per cent in military spending, with resources redirected to development purposes. On a more modest scale, Kazakhstan's President Nursultan Nazarbayev has called for all countries to donate 1 per cent of their military spending to the United Nations Special Fund for Global Development.

PLAN

To introduce an international 2.5 per cent tax on all transactions will require a massive public campaign on the inhuman consequences of the arms trade, plus lobbying at both supply and demand levels over at least 5 years for disinvestment, plus public demonstrations in the capitals of all 6 largest arms exporting countries.

....

17. Defuse our violent response to terrorism

PRINCIPLE

Adopt fair and peaceful processes instead of violent reaction. The most inclusive, effective approach governments and corporations can take to defuse international terrorism will be to immediately adopt genuinely fair and peaceful processes in their dealings with other peoples. This strategy would deprive terror groups of one of their most compelling justifications for violence.[102]

Current methods for dealing with terrorism are simply repeating previous grave errors of decision-making that exacerbate the problem. In order to map an effective strategy it is vital to understand how militant fighters think, and what they fear.

To respond to terrorism with violence is counter-productive, because violence is what terrorists understand, and they are masters of exploiting our addiction to news of their brutality. Violence, says former Islamic State captive Nicolas Hénin, is exactly what his captors want: "They will be heartened by every sign of overreaction, of division, of fear, of racism, of xenophobia; they will be drawn to any examples of ugliness on social media." [103]

Deeyah Khan is an Emmy award-winning documentary film-maker whose most recent project, *Jihad*, involved two years of interviews and filming with former Islamic extremists. She says that their mission "is aimed at breaking the world into two opposed camps, jihadis and crusaders, locked in an apocalyptic battle, that fits into their own, reductive world view... The Islamic State does not want us to open our doors to their refugees. It wants them to be hopeless and desperate. It does not want us to enjoy ourselves with our families and friends in bars and concert halls, stadiums and restaurants. It wants us to huddle in our houses, within our own social groups, and close our doors in fear."[104]

EXAMPLE

Since Islamist terror groups portray the West as anti-Islam, welcoming migrants is a direct antidote to their strategy. The German example is the most powerful respnse to date. Although Angela Merkel initially suffered in opinion polls after her welcome to refugees, her actions were a signal example of how to defuse ISIS rhetoric that the West hates Islam.
If the West wants to dissuade young, disaffected people from joining a violent jihad against it, then it has to prove — and not merely declare — that it cares about their relative poverty and political exclusion. In May 2016 UNHCR reported that $1.65 billion was still needed to co-ordinate accommodation for nearly 5 million refugees. The US alone had by then spent four times that sum — $6.4 billion — on bombing ISIS.[105]

PLAN

Defuse our violent response to terrorism by positive welcoming of migrants. Encourage and support governments to publicise the welcome of refugees and migrants and the refusal of citizens to stay at home and limit their activities because of fear.

18. Deprive terrorism of the oxygen of publicity

PRINCIPLE

A co-ordinated plan to educate media is required. Nothing should be done which supports the image of the terrorist as a heroic warrior defending the interests of the people. Incidents like Abu Ghraib, tank shells fired into the Gaza strip and the vast personal coverage of the Paris bombers, all made it easier for militants to claim convincingly that their campaign of violence, repugnant to so many outsiders, is not only legitimate amongst Muslims, but noble.

When western media consistently feature terrorists on their front pages, giving them quasi-populist names like 'Jihadi John', they can see themselves as global celebrities. Other young men then naturally crave such oxygen of publicity, even if it costs them their lives.

EXAMPLE

In July 2016 France's largest and most respected news outlets refused to publish the names and photos of terrorists in a campaign against 'glorification' amid a wave of Isis-inspired attacks. It will be interesting to observe which major news outlets will follow France's example and deny airspace to terrorism.

PLAN

Western leaders to orchestrate a cohesive and co-ordinated programme to educate media editors why featuring portraits and biographies of suicide bombers simply gives airspace to Jihad. The opposite — denying airspace — would work far better to minimise the glamour of brutality.

....

19. Global Peace Index — top ten to invest

PRINCIPLE

The Global Peace Index measures the relative position of nations' and regions' peacefulness. Developed in consultation with an international panel of peace experts from peace institutes and think tanks with data collected and collated by the Economist Intelligence Unit, the list was launched in May 2007 and updated annually. The index gauges global peace using three broad themes: the level of safety and security in society, the extent of domestic and international conflict, and the degree of militarisation. In the top ten most peaceful nations, the Index demonstrates the advantages of peace for prosperity; the last ten nations in the Index show starkly how armed violence correlates precisely with poverty.

After successfully building two international software companies, Steve Killelea decided to dedicate most of his time and fortune to sustainable development and peace. In 2007 he founded the Institute for Economics and Peace (IEP), an international think tank dedicated to building a greater understanding of the interconnection between business, peace and economics with particular emphasis on the economic benefits of peace. IEP have the goal of educating one million people globally on positive peace. "By becoming more knowledgeable about peace, we believe that young people will be better prepared to help shape a better future for the planet. This training program is in its final stages of development, and we expect to start rolling it out early in the new year."

EXAMPLE

Britain, the EU and the World Bank are helping to fund a job creation project in Ethiopia that will involve the building of two industrial centres at a cost of $500m. These should provide 100,000 jobs, around a third of which would go to refugees. Although these bodies are not in the GPI top ten, their action is just one of many that show how the wealthy can assist and support poorer nations to escape the cycle of violence.

PLAN

The ten countries at the top of the Index, who have discovered the advantages of investing in a peaceful society, be encouraged by Steve Kilellea and the Institute for Economics and Peace to invest in the ten least peaceful countries in the world. They would do this by enabling political leaders in the top ten to support the leaders of those poorer countries, their business leaders to assist with investment there and their entrepreneurs to inspire projects to multiply opportunities.

---

20. Youth employment in the Middle East

PRINCIPLE

Devise effective systems to train unemployed youth in the Middle East and North Africa (MENA) region to support rural populations to become self-sufficient in food, water and energy production.

With 40 million unemployed youth and 27 million not in education, employment, or training, the MENA region has the highest rate of youth unemployment in the world at 27.2 per cent, according to the World Economic Forum. This presents a serious problem for a region where more than half the 369 million inhabitants are under the age of 25. Due to a sharp decline in oil prices over the past 15 months, unemployment levels in the oil-exporting countries in the region are expected to surge as governments are poised to cut spending to cope with rising fiscal deficits.[106]

If just a small percentage of the region's underemployed were trained as social entrepreneurs to work in rural areas with the explicit task of devising and enacting localised schemes, they could:

- Resurrect agricultural techniques to produce food supplies locally, re-using seed banks and storage capacities, thus cutting transportation costs;
- Introduce measures to produce reliable supplies of potable water; for example in 2016 Israel revealed that it now produces 55% of its freshwater, meaning that one of the driest countries on earth now has more water than it needs;
- Set up renewable energy production.

EXAMPLE

Sinal do Vale is an innovative organic farm in Brazil, a reforestation and community resilience project, a living laboratory for the transition to sustainability. Sinal is a catalyst for tangible social and environmental change both locally and globally, providing social entrepreneurs, students and volunteers from all over the world with a space for dialogue and practical experimentation in the field of sustainability.[107]

PLAN

10 per cent of the 67 million underemployed in the MENA region to be trained as social entrepreneurs to support rural areas to produce food supplies locally, develop reliable supplies of potable water, and set up renewable energy production, principally solar, now available at very low rates. Such systems would serve not only to provide employment, but also to reduce economic migration to urban areas and to the West. Local Sharia Funds would be ideal as local investors for this kind of initiative.

....

21. The Sunni-Shia divide

PRINCIPLE

Given the disastrous proxy war in Syria, it may now be possible to build support for sufficient numbers of clerics on both sides to work together for shared Muslim values, rather than fighting to be right over their differing rituals and interpretation of Islamic law.

There have been efforts by Sunni and Shia clerics to reduce tensions through dialogue and counter-violence measures, on the basis that when human beings sit down and talk to each other, they learn to respect each other. Quran teachings would seem to support this:

- Dialogue allows parties to understand each other better by allowing participants to acquire direct knowledge about beliefs instead of relying on propaganda and stereotypical images. (Quran 49:6–12)
- Dialogue will isolate the extremist fringe. It is a major sin to kill a human being. Killing a human being is like killing the whole of humanity. By talking to each other, Shias and Sunnis will be able to save lives, which is like saving the whole of humanity. (Quran 5:32)
- Even if some Shias and Sunnis consider each other enemies, the Quran asks us to be just even toward one's enemy: "O you who believe! Stand out firmly for God, as witnesses to fair dealing, and let not the hatred of others to you make you swerve to wrong and depart from justice. Be just: that is next to Piety: and fear Allah. For Allah is well-acquainted with all that you do." (Quran 5:8)[108]

EXAMPLE

In the 1960s in Pakistan, when Shia-Sunni fights were far less significant, city officers used to convene joint meetings of Shia and Sunni leaders to chalk out Muharram plans so no confusion would result in rioting. These government-arranged dialogues helped keep conflicts at a minimum. Considering the current level of mistrust, it will be beneficial if civil society takes initiatives for dialogue at all levels of society.[109]

PLAN

Dialogues to be organised in Muslim communities across the planet, to include Imams and caretakers of Masjids, national level religious leadership and Shia and Sunni businesspersons including women. Muslim women globally[110] could collaborate between their organisations to support this kind of initiative.

....

22. Early warning systems that work

PRINCIPLE

Efficient early warning, whether by grassroots intelligence, internet co-ordination or by complex radar systems, is clearly vital to the prevention of armed conflict. Far more attention must be paid to these early warning signs of armed violence.

The Armed Conflict Location & Event Data Project is the most comprehensive public collection of political violence and protest data for developing states. Information is recorded on the battles, killings, riots, and recruitment activities of rebels, governments, militias, armed groups, protesters and civilians.[111]

The Early Warning Project blog also provides regular analysis of at-risk countries and evolving situations, used to track ongoing events, to call out related research and advocacy, and to hear from guest bloggers and interviewees with expertise on early warning or prevention in specific countries and regions.[112] Far more attention must be paid to these early warning signs of armed violence. Teams of trained mediators need to be ready to move at short notice to move into an area at risk and work with local expertise on a viable prevention plan.

EXAMPLE

Leymah Gbowee led a women's peace movement that helped bring an end to the Second Liberian Civil War in 2003, for which she was awarded the Nobel Peace Prize.[113] She wrote: "We were being trained to use a conflict prevention tool called 'early warners'. It was a way of teaching activists how to draw on local people's observations of odd events or behaviours to spot a problem brewing, then come up with strategies to defuse it. For example, the market women might notice the unusual presence of many men, strange men, on market day, a sign that fighters had come to town and a battle was about to erupt."

PLAN

A super-efficient early warning system for the prevention of conflict be set up without delay, using an automated computer system to include keyword searches of websites and social networks and assessing the developments in the deep web, to create a graphics-based early warning 'barometer' for emerging conflicts, continuously vetted by journalists and experts in the signs of erupting armed conflict. All the bodies mentioned in this chapter — the UN, governments, international non governmental organisations, locally led peace builders and other civil society organisations — to be linked in to the early warning system, to co-ordinate and streamline their actions.

Leymah Gbowee

23. Early intervention

PRINCIPLE

The earliest of 'early interventions' is of course prevention, and the key to prevention is the crucial role of dialogue in intervening in a conflict situation before it even gets off the ground.

For obvious reasons it is hard to measure the effects of early intervention, since it would involve an attempt to quantify events that did not happen because they were effectively prevented. But there are situations where we can make an informed judgment. One distinctly measurable case is that of the post-election violence in Kenya in 2008, resulting in some 1,500 deaths and as many as 250,000 displaced, as compared to the subsequent elections of 2013, when in addition to legal reforms, locally-led conflict prevention teams were trained and in place, as well as substantial community peace-building initiatives. There was little violence in 2013 and no deaths.

EXAMPLE

The Oxford Process has a unique and niche methodology. Its approach to preventing conflicts is working quietly behind the scenes with adversaries with the aim, wherever possible, of bringing these together around a table in a structured and safe environment to ripen the conditions for official negotiations. Over a 30-year period Oxford Research Group facilitated discussions between Chinese, French and Soviet nuclear weapons decision-makers and their US and British counterparts, on issues of fissile materials and nuclear proliferation.

PLAN

Assemble five teams of trained mediators to be ready to move at short notice into an area at risk and work with local expertise on a viable prevention plan. Initiatives such as the Oxford Process require sustained funding, not only to train mediators from different regions and ethnicities, but to cover the expenses of early intervention.

"Dekha Ibrahim Abdi, whose pioneering work in Kenya helped train the locally-led community peace-building initiatives to prevent violence during the 2013 Kenyan elections, even after her death."

24. Engage corporate leaders in the business of peace

PRINCIPLE

To persuade private business that it has a public role, in peace as in war. Corporate Social Responsibility cannot any longer confine itself to recycling, fair trade and ethical sourcing for products, because armed conflicts are increasingly affecting trading operations. Moreover the moral and ethical reasons for business leaders to wake up to their potential role in peace-building are now obvious.

Jane Nelson is senior fellow/director of the Corporate Social Responsibility Initiative, Harvard JFK School of Government. Drawing on examples from over 30 countries and from a variety of industry sectors, the report addresses both the positive and negative roles that business can play in situations of conflict, showing why the private sector can no longer afford to ignore the causes and costs of conflict. It demonstrates how business can play a negative role by creating or exacerbating violent conflict, or a positive role by helping to prevent or resolve it; and the practical actions that companies can undertake, with an imperative for action.[114]

EXAMPLE

There are thousands of examples worldwide where businesses have undertaken reforestation and re-greening of the desert, but here is just one: SEKEM is a 60 hectare farm north-east of Cairo, previously desert but now growing varieties of herbs for a highly profitable tea company. SEKEM teaches conflict prevention in its schools and trains 600 farmers from the Nile delta in organic vegetable production, exporting to supermarkets in Europe. This business has become highly profitable and inspired similar initiatives in other areas affected by drought.

PLAN

CEOs and finance directors the world over to be alerted to the practical actions that their companies can take to improve peaceful relations in the areas where they operate, and to prevent armed conflict. The UN

Global Compact to increase its research into the cost-effectiveness of corporate investment in peace-building and conflict prevention, and also to build a campaign to publicise the business advantages — especially for shipping, tourism and insurance industries — of ensuring peaceful environments. The World Economic Forum at Davos to run a major annual session with workshops, clear outcomes and undertakings to ensure corporate engagement beyond traditional CSR.

25. Copy Bhutan's example of Gross National Happiness

PRINCIPLE

The Gross National Happiness Index is a single number index developed from 33 indicators categorised under nine domains. These indicators to be used to create policy incentives for the government, NGOs and businesses worldwide to increase GNH.

GNH is a term coined by the King of Bhutan in the 1970s to mean "the peace and happiness of our people and the security and sovereignty of the nation". The concept implies that sustainable development should take a holistic approach towards notions of progress and give equal importance to non-economic aspects of wellbeing. The nine domains of GNH values are: psychological wellbeing, health, education, time use, cultural diversity and resilience, good governance, community vitality, ecological diversity and resilience, and living standards.

EXAMPLE

Bhutan[115] has pledged to remain carbon neutral for all time, with the mission to put happiness before economic growth and set a world standard for environmental preservation. Bhutan isn't just carbon neutral — it's carbon negative; Gross National Happiness ('development with values') is more important than Gross National Product.[116]

By 2020 Bhutan will be exporting enough electricity to offset 17 million tons of CO2; Bhutan achieves this by providing free electricity to rural farmers so farmers do not need firewood to cook food; subsidising costs of LED lights; 'Green Bhutan', a project to plant trees throughout the country; more than half of the country is 'protected areas' (national parks, wild life sanctuaries, nature reserves) and they are all connected to each other through a network of biological corridors, i.e. animals are free to move everywhere.

PLAN

The Bhutanese government to be subsidised to invite leaders of 10 countries each year for ten years to witness the physical and psychological advantages for its people of its national GNH plan.

....

The next chapter translates each of these twenty-five Plans into an itemised costing, and estimates the total cost of a Business Plan for Peace based on systems that effectively prevent conflict and build peace at local, national and international levels.

If a pragmatic approach can be adopted that links local, national, regional and global objectives into a whole system, it will be possible to transform the twenty-first century into a century of peace.

Chapter 5

Costing the Business Plan for Peace

To date, as far as I know, no one has produced a Business Plan for Peace, based on systems that effectively prevent conflict and build peace at local, national and international levels. In order to enable readers to envisage a different kind of future, the Plan below is based on different assumptions from those underpinning current decisions of governments. The first new assumption concerns the power and cost effectiveness of the prevention of armed conflict; the second concerns the emerging potential to use a tax on arms trading to pay for the building of peace at local, national and international levels.

T his Plan is unprecedented, and these figures are illustrative of the order of magnitude of the task. The figures given are derived from existing examples and experience of costings where possible, based on the experience of professionals in the field, but some are of necessity approximations, given that a number of the plans proposed are new. In each case they are are based on a 10-year estimate. At the end of the chapter some current global spending figures are presented for purposes of comparison.

As in the previous chapter the Business Plan starts with the methods found to be most effective at local levels, followed by what can best be done by national governments, concluding with the systems that work best at a global level.

The Institute for Economics and Peace, in an invaluable initiative, has constructed a global model of peacebuilding cost–effectiveness, concluding that increased funding for peacebuilding would be hugely beneficial not only to peacebuilding outcomes but in terms of the potential economic returns to the global economy. The total peace dividend the international community would reap if it doubled peacebuilding commitments over the next ten years is calculated to be US$2.94 trillion.[117] It is important to note that the IEP study deals with aspects of conflict mitigation and post conflict reconstruction, whereas the plan outlined in this chapter is confined to the prevention of armed conflict.

Systems that effectively prevent conflict and build peace at local levels

PLAN
1. Funding to be made available to at least 1,400 effective locally led peace-building organisations across 44 different conflict-affected regions, for a period of 10 years
2. Six regional platforms to be set up to administer funding to locally-led initiatives and conduct monitoring and evaluation
3. Break the cycle of violence by encouraging new local systems to provide physical, political and psychological security through tried and tested methods of conflict prevention
4. Widespread training schemes to be set up to share knowledge of how trauma counselling works, and to adapt and develop practices suited to different cultures. This can be carried out by trauma counselling organisations — such as the International Association of Trauma Professionals — setting up 'out-reach training' in appropriate languages

ITEMISATION	COST
1400 organisations each receive $10k annually for 10 years	**$140,000,000**
Establish 6 regional platforms @ $50,000: $300,000. Admin of same over 10 years @ $100,000 pa: $6m	**$6,300,000**
Support 100 new peace-building organisations per annum @ $10k & continue support for 10 years	**$10,000,000**
Training schemes centred on 6 regional platforms @ $50,000 pa for 10 years	**$3,000,000**
Total costs of systems to prevent conflict at local levels	$159,300,000

Systems for preventing conflict at national/regional levels

PLAN

5. Ten governments to build national Infrastructures for Peace by recruiting respected community leaders to join Peace Councils at national, regional, city, town and village levels; they are trained in violence prevention methods and required to develop a Peace Plan for their area, should violence break out

6. Enable qualified women to fill policy-making roles on peace & security through research that presents profiles of suitably qualified women in 30 conflict affected countries to relevant authorities, and lobby for their acceptance in policy-making roles and negotiations

7. Women's organisations in every country or region at risk of violent extremism to receive funding to learn from the methods employed by Kongira Star and other similar initiatives

8. Truth and Reconciliation Commissions to be set up in 4 regions or countries that have undergone historic or recent extreme violations of human rights, such as Northern Ireland or Colombia, in order to prevent the repetition of the cycle of violence

9. The UN and NATO to set standards for all member nations to establish Conflict Prevention funds with a requirement that these funds amount to a specific per cent of their defence budget

ITEMISATION	COST
Costs of training to set up I4P in 10 countries @ $2m = $20m. Costs of maintenance @ $1m pa = $10m x 10 years = $100m	$120,000,000
Present profiles of 30 suitably qualified women in 30 conflict affected countries to relevant authorities = (30 x 30) x $500 = $450,000, and lobby for their acceptance in policy-making roles and negotiations	$450,000
Support for women's organisations in 30 countries at risk of violent extremism = 30 x $500,000pa for 10 years = $150m	$150,000,000
Canadian TRC cost approx. $6m, so approx. cost for 4 countries = $24m	$24,000,000
Countries to be lobbied and encouraged by the UN and NATO (where relevant) to step up and annually increase their funding for the prevention of conflict. Lobbying costs: $1m pa for 10 years	$10,000,000

PLAN

10. Produce and implement strategies for diversification: the ingenuity of engineers now employed in the arms industry is redeployed to turn the UK into a world leader in green technology

11. A major campaign to persuade pension and sovereign wealth funds to divest from arms production and invest in innovative financing linked to renewable energy, beneficial to individuals and communities

12. Multi-Stakeholder Dialogue to take place every 2 years between the main actors in the peace-building field, to discuss the principle causes of violent conflict and how they can most effectively be addressed

13. Provide the world's 10 most conflict-affected countries — Libya, Sudan, Ukraine, Central African Republic, Yemen, Somalia, Afghanistan, Iraq, South Sudan, Syria — **with a Peace Building in each country**

ITEMISATION	COST
Commission 10 university departments assisted by unions to develop viable strategies for diversification for top 10 UK arms manufacturing companies = 10 x $1m = $10m. Press and media coverage for same = 10 x $500,000 = $5m	**$15,000,000**
Multi-faceted campaign via major investment advisers and parliamentary representatives to encourage pension funds to divest from arms production and invest in renewables	**$90,000,000**
Dialogues to take place every 2 years at an annual cost of $1m (preparation, travel & accommodation, reports, facilitation, security etc) = $5m over 10 years	**$5,000,000**
Ten peace buildings @ approx. $25m each = $250m	**$250,000,000**
Total costs of systems to prevent conflict at national/regional levels	$664,450,000

Systems for preventing conflict at international levels

PLAN

14. Civil society organisations to engage with the UN to support Plan 16 for a global brake on the arms trade, and divert part of the 10 per cent tax to fund the **UN Emergency Peace Service**

15. Five regional mediator teams to be set up in five distinct regions, to include representatives of relevant cultures, ethnicities and belief systems, trained and resourced to become available at short notice

16. Campaign for global brake on arms trading, to introduce an international 2.5 per cent tax on all arms sales and transactions

17. Defuse our violent response to terrorism by positive welcoming of refugees and migrants. Encourage and support governments to publicise the welcome of refugees and the refusal of citizens to stay at home and limit their activities because of fear

18. Deprive terrorism of the oxygen of publicity by a coordinated programme to educate media editors why featuring portraits and biographies of suicide bombers simply gives airspace to Jihad

ITEMISATION	COST
Support for civil society organisations to work with allies in the UN and interested governments; pump-prime funding to 10 existing civil society organisations @ $100,000 pa for 10 years	**$10,000,000**
Establish 5 regional teams ready trained @ $200,000 per team. Expenses of intervention @ average $1m by three teams pa for 10 years = $30m	**$31,000,000**
Stage 1: massive publicity campaign and public discussion on the ethics and viability of the arms trade. Stage 2: lobbying at both supply and demand level for 5 years @ $5m. Stage 3: public demonstration in 6 capitals calling for divestment @ $1m	Stage 1: $5m Stage 2: $25m Stage 3: $6m **Total:** **$36,000,000**
Provide funding for documentary films showing benefits of welcoming and integrating refugees and migrants: 5 films @ $50,000 in each of 5 countries	**$1,250,000**
Co-ordinate 5-year government campaigns in 5 countries subject to terror attacks to educate media to ban photos and 'air-time' for terrorists. $5m pa for 5 years	**$25,000,000**

PLAN

19. Global Peace Index: The ten countries at the top of the Index, who have discovered the advantages of investing in a peaceful society, to invest in the ten least peaceful countries in the world, encouraging their own political leaders to support the leaders of those poorer countries, their business leaders to assist with investment there and their entrepreneurs to inspire projects to multiply employment opportunities

20. Youth employment in the Middle East: 10 per cent of the 67 million underemployed youth in the MENA region to be trained as social entrepreneurs to support rural populations to become self-sufficient in food, water and energy production

21. The Sunni-Shia divide. Dialogues to be organised in Muslim communities across the planet, to include Imams and caretakers of Masjids, national level religious leadership, and Shia and Sunni businesspersons including women

22. Early warning systems that work. A super-efficient early warning system for the prevention of conflict to be set up without delay, using an automated computer system to include keyword searches of websites and social networks, to create a graphics-based early warning 'barometer' for emerging conflicts, continuously vetted by journalists and experts in the signs of erupting armed conflict

23. Assemble five teams of trained mediators to be ready to move at short notice into an area at risk and work with local expertise on a viable prevention plan. Initiatives such as the Oxford Process require sustained funding, not only to train mediators from different regions and ethnicities, but to cover the expenses of early intervention

ITEMISATION	COST
Work with Institute for Economics & Peace to prepare 10 briefings at $500,000 each. International lobbying to persuade 10 countries to invest $3m pa over 5 years = $15m	**$20,000,000**
Training schemes in 10 MENA countries for 6.7 million underemployed youth @ $10m per country for 5 years = $500,000,000. Support for approx. 6000 self-sufficiency projects @ $5,000 pa for 10 years = $300m. Total: $800m	**$800,000,000**
Global campaign by moderate Muslim organisations world-wide to encourage dialogues between religious leaders, supported by Muslim women's organisations. Communications support = $9m	**$9,000,000**
Develop the existing concept = $400,000. Publicise and extend access to local sources, correspondents to verify information = $500,000. Maintain for 10 years @ $500,000pa = $5m	**$5,400,000**
Extend the Oxford Process to have 5 teams ready trained @ $200,000 per team = $1m. Expenses of intervention @ average $1m by three teams pa for 10 years = $30m	**$31,000,000**

PLAN

24. CEOs and finance directors the world over to be alerted to the practical actions that their companies can take to improve peaceful relations in the areas where they operate, and to prevent armed conflict. The UN Global Compact to increase its research into the cost-effectiveness of corporate investment in peace-building and conflict prevention, and build a campaign to publicise the business advantages

25. The Bhutanese government to be subsidised to invite leaders of 10 countries each year for ten years to witness the physical and psychological advantages for its people of its Gross National Happiness plan

ITEMISATION	COST
UN Global compact research costs @ $5m for 5 years = $25m. Campaign to publicise business advantages worldwide @ $5m for 5 years = $25m	**$50,000,000**
Costs of 10 leaders invited to witness Bhutanese GNH @ $1m for 10 years = $100m	**$100,000,000**
Total cost of systems for preventing conflict at international levels	$1,118,650,000

Total cost of local, national and international systems for preventing conflict over a 10-year period:

$1,942,400,000

Cost comparison

For purposes of comparison, in April 2017 SIPRI estimated that global military expenditure in 2016 was $1686 billion. That is just for one year. With a world population of 7.6 billion,[118] this equals to $221.8 for every person on the planet.

The above calculation to bring a global Peace Plan into action is estimated to cost $1,942,400,000 for ten years, just under two billion, or approx. $194,240,000 for one year. With a world population of 7,600,000,000, **this equals just under 3 cents for every person on the planet.**

This is a very small amount, concentrating only on known and viable initiatives. The costs of addressing the root causes of conflict — namely climate change, the rich-poor divide, migration, overpopulation and terrorism — must be considered.

Other comparisons:

* The decommissioning costs of the Fukushima reactors (a multiple meltdown in March 2011) will top $105 billion.[119]
* Yearly we spend $59 billion on ice cream alone.
* Proctor & Gamble spent $9.3 billion on advertising in 2012.

Where would the funds come from?

As we have seen, a 2.5 per cent tax levied on current annual arms sales ($94.5 billion) would yield approximately $2,350,000,000. This revenue would be invested in addressing the root causes of conflict, including the 25 Plans formulated above. If the plan to levy a tax on arms sales did not materialise, then the funds for the 25 Plans can be raised from minute contributions as a percentage of the 'defence' budgets of UN member states. If for example Japan can find $105 billion for efforts to clean up the Fukushima disaster, the country can certainly contribute 1 per cent ($4,200,000)of its defence budget at $42 billion in 2015.

Preventing violence at source

What is obvious, of course, is that given our present way of thinking, the issue is 'security' rather than comparative costs. So how could humanity learn that safety and security lie in preventing violence at source, rather than waiting until armed conflict has broken out, and then attempting to pick up the pieces?

If that is the argument we need to have, we should apply our proposed plan to a recent example such as Syria.

Syria

We shall examine whether, if some of the ideas above had been applied, the brutality and chaos of the Syrian war might have been prevented. As we've seen, the first underlying principle in the prevention strategy is respect, the second is that prevention takes place early in the conflict, and the third concerns the use of power with others, rather than power over others.

Protests began in Syria as early as 26 January 2011, calling for democracy, an end to the state of emergency in force since 1963, and an end to corruption. On 17 February at a demonstration in Damascus in protest at police beating a shop keeper, protesters chanted: "the Syrian people will not be humiliated". After many other protests, on 15 March 2011 a 'Day of Rage' took place, generally considered to mark the start of a nationwide uprising. The reaction of the Syrian regime, already terrified by what had happened to the leadership in Egypt and Tunisia, became violent on 16 March, and deadly on 18 March, when four unarmed protesters were killed in Daraa.

In February and the first half of March, if the Syrian leadership had recognised the protest and indicated some willingness to listen to demands, a different scenario would have developed. This would have required expert mediators, first to sit with all parties to understand their demands and fears, and then to propose terms for a series of meetings between the regime and the leadership of the protests, upholding the principle of respect for all sides.

While early intervention at a local level would have been of key importance, mediation at government level between Syria and the leadership of other countries would have been critical. This needed to happen before this 'internal' conflict could be inflamed by those tempted to engage in proxy wars in the region. Thus the deployment of independent mediator teams would have been vital, able to respond with speed and agility and not get caught in the quagmire of bureaucracies.

They would have liaised quietly and below the radar with governments having interests in the conflict, and would have fed back signs of the kind of emerging scenarios that have now proved so disastrous in Syrian war. This would have enabled wiser discussion and decisions within the United Nations and between Permanent Members of the Security Council.

Such teams would have included nationals of the surrounding areas where conflict was brewing or already inflamed, who would be best placed to explain the realities on the ground and the perceptions and attitudes of the stakeholders concerned.

Drought and the uprising

Drawing one of the strongest links yet between global warming and human conflict, in a study published in March 2015 in the Proceedings of the US National Academy of Sciences, researchers said that an extreme drought in Syria between 2006 and 2009 was most likely due to climate change, and that the drought was a factor in the vio-lent uprising that began there in 2011.[120] The drought caused many frustrated farmers to migrate to cities, where their anger helped fuel the protests. Again, if the regime had taken pre-emptive actions to meet the needs of farmers, this anger could have been mitigated (see Plan 20 in Chapter 4).

Civil society

It would likewise have been extremely useful if the skills of Syrian civil society had been engaged at an early stage, since the organisations that have evolved over recent decades are sophisticated and knowledgeable. Citizens for Syria has mapped 1,012 viable organisations (of which 114 were in Aleppo) and given detailed results of the 837 they were able to verify. The data is presented in an interactive map, various charts and a table with an advanced search function.[121]

If the Syrian regime had identified some of these civil society organisations with whom it could negotiate at an early stage in the conflict, those organisations would have conveyed the needs of the Syrian people in a rational way that would have allowed for compromises to be reached.

To guage the dedication, skill and sheer courage of Syrian civil society as it has had to develop in the war, the White Helmets are a good example. Since there are no ambulance or fire services in parts of Syria to rescue people when the barrel bombs fall, the White Helmets go in with their makeshift vehicles. They risk the 'double tap' — aircraft returning to bomb those who try to help the wounded; 141 White Helmets have been killed saving lives. If the Syrian regime had been willing to accept offers of mediation in the early days of the conflict, the lives of these magnificent men and women would not have been lost, and could have been devoted to building a safe and prosperous Syria (see Plans 7, 12 and 14 in Chapter 4).

Ashraf is a 27-year-old former Syrian Air Force pilot who flew MIG fighters until he took the decision to refuse an order to bomb civilians. He speaks matter-of-factly: "When I was released from prison after two years, I weighed 30 kilos and had to spend five months in hospital recovering." Leaving hospital and looking around at the destruction, he met one of the White Helmets and decided to establish a Civil Defence centre in Latakia. When asked if he feels fear when running towards collapsing buildings, he says "Of course. But we know those people in there need us. What I'm really afraid of is finding dead children."[122]

Birds fly over the destroyed houses in
Khalidiya district in Homs, Syria

The role of Syrian women

Women's peace-building efforts and activities are undertaken in areas controlled by all warring parties to the conflict, and cover issues including:
- Promoting civil peace and coexistence (Aleppo, northern Syria);
- Combating child recruitment (Deir Ezzor, eastern Syria);
- Raising awareness on consequences of violence (Al-Hasaka, northeastern Syria);
- Building transitional justice mechanisms (Damascus and its countryside)

The Badael report, *Peace-building defines our future now* (2015), provides a unique observation into women's peacemaking activism efforts inside Syria.[123]

Although the ongoing militarisation of the conflict in Syria constitutes the main and most threatening challenge to women's peace-building efforts, lack of funding, as reported in the Badael report, is "the overall main reason behind activities being terminated". In addition, there is acute need for staff training, specifically in political, social and economic empowerment.

This is where the on-line activist community could have helped, for example by calling for a guarantee that women's groups and activists were included in the peace process substantively and at all levels. For the future "This implies shifting the narrow focus on national and international formal negotiations to a broader peace-building framework that encompasses inclusive and diverse apparatuses, beyond the obsolete male-dominated processes." The change of discourse on women's participation must be shifted from a normative "why participate?" to a practical and efficient "how to participate?" This has to come from a genuine recognition of them as influential peace-builders without whom the peace process is not only incomplete, but also unsustainable (see Plans 6 and 7 in Chapter 4).

Unemployment

The underlying problem in Syria — as in much of the Middle East — is of a marginalised majority, many of whom are unemployed graduates with no job prospects. Therefore if our strategy had been applied, whereby the ten countries at the top of the Global Peace Index who have discovered the advantages of investing in a peaceful society, had invested in Syria, Lebanon, Tunisia and other Magreb countries, things would look very different by now. Their political leaders would have supported and advised the leaders of those poorer countries, their business leaders would have assisted with investment and their entrepreneurs would have inspired projects to multiply employment opportunities (see Plan 20 in Chapter 4).

Against a backdrop of bomb blasts by militant group al-Shabaab, 116 young people in Somalia recently overcame a past torn apart by clan violence. They have just graduated from a six-month skills training course learning to become electricians, plumbers and tailors. This is part of a three-year project to support livelihoods, improve job creation and help build peace between previously warring communities. For Abdifatah, the training altered the course of his life: "Before I joined the vocational training, my ambition was to join the boat migration to Europe. How to migrate and reach Europe was my biggest worry. But today such worries have vanished. I am a skilled person and can create my own business." [124]

No-fly zone

Even at a much later stage in the conflict, the international community could have paid heed to the many calls for a no-fly zone. One such call came from a clearly non-partisan collaboration between the Jews for Human Rights in Syria, in solidarity with the Syrian American Council and the Coalition for a Democratic Syria. In January 2015 they called for the United States and its international partners "to immediately establish a coalition for a No-Fly Zone in Syrian airspace. A No-Fly Zone will protect civilians merely trying to survive the inhumanity of constant regime barrel bombs, which are the main killers of Syrian civilians. Stopping the killing must be a priority. Although our groups come from different faith traditions, our goal is just and clear: all life is worth protecting, no matter the cost."[125]

The United Nations

Despite many efforts, the United Nations has shown its internal organisation to be paralysed over Syria, with Permanent Members of the Security Council consistently blocking efforts to negotiate, allow safe passage or even establish cease-fires. It showed itself unable to prevent what became a killing field in Aleppo.

This shameful indictment of the 'international community' clearly indicates the urgent need for UN structural reform. The organisation requires immediate overhaul to include the Security Council being composed of members with equal voting powers and not subject to 'one country veto'. The bureaucracy of the UN also requires substantial over-haul to release it from the stultifying and dated procedures of the past and introduce stream-lined decision-making processes made possible by 21st-century technology.

If, and only if, such structural reform takes place, there is a strong case for the UN to establish an umbrella organisation for peace-building, to undertake co-ordination of the 10 per cent tax to be levied on current annual arms sales and devoted to the funding and administration of some aspects of the above Business Plan.

PART THREE: WHO CAN DO THIS, AND HOW?

Chapter 6

The Rise in Citizen Action

The exponential rise in local initiatives

Too often political leaders say that the complex decisions involved in armed conflict situations require skilled professional diplomacy and make painful compromise inevitable. In the world of realpolitik, the argument runs, pragmatism will always trump idealism.

From the perspective of those working for peace worldwide, that argument looks like a failure of imagination. "Lasting resolutions require far more effort than just a politician's signature on a treaty; the peace processes that work are founded on a broad spectrum of initiatives in which citizens play a full part."[126]

Those filtered to the top by our current political systems tend by nature to be better at argument, competition and aggression than listening, mediation and compassion. That's the name of the game, currently. And that's why attempts to stop war from the top down are so prone to failure. Syria is a current example.

So something different is required. And in my observation something different is happening. We have already seen that locally-led initiatives to prevent conflict in the most violent parts of the world have increased four-fold, and we have become familiar with the incredible courage of people risking their lives to stop war at the sharp end.

At the same time a vast energy for change has been emerging from the ground up, right across the planet, reported by Paul Hawken in his book *Blessed Unrest* in 2007. He charted "how the largest social movement in the world came into being, and why no one saw it coming".

Hawken spent over a decade researching organisations dedicated to restoring the environment and fostering social justice. From billion-dollar nonprofits to single-person causes, in his view these groups collectively comprise the largest movement on earth, a movement that has no name, leader, or location, and that has gone largely ignored by politicians and the media. "Like nature itself, it is organising from the bottom up, in every city, town, and culture and is emerging to be an extraordinary and creative expression of people's needs worldwide."

As just one example of how this phenomenon has grown since Hawken published in 2007, a decade has seen the Transition movement grow from just two groups in 2006 (Kinsale, Ireland and Totnes, England) to initiatives in more than 43 countries across the world, with 1,258 Transition Towns registered in the UK alone by April 2016. The terms transition town, transition initiative and transition model refer to grassroot community projects that aim to increase self-sufficiency to reduce the potential effects of peak oil, climate destruction, and economic instability.

The values of Millennials and social entrepreneurs

Surveys by Goldman Sachs and KPMG have begun to chart the values of Millennials. By 2020, those born between 1980 and 2000 will form 50 per cent of the global workforce and will be the largest consumer class. Attracting and keeping Millennials is apparently giving many CEOs sleepless nights. Why? "Because an overwhelming 75 per cent of us believe that businesses are focused on their own agendas rather than helping to improve society."

It appears that Millennials have four major priorities: PLANET, PEOPLE, PURPOSE & PROFIT.[127] An enormous number of Millennials worldwide consider environmental protection, addressing climate change, resource scarcity and biodiversity loss as their No.1 Priority. The second concerns people: inequality of income and wealth and unemployment are the next concerns that Millennials raise.

Thirdly, purpose: personal and professional development, coaching and learning are important for more than fifty per cent of Millennials. They prefer to work with organisations that are ethical, transparent and investing in their staff. Lastly, profit is the lowest priority for most

Millennials globally. They only consider it important in as far as it sustains their cost and standard of living.

I encounter exactly this growing phenomenon in my work with young social entrepreneurs. Just one example of many: the DO School[128] for social entrepreneurs began life in Hamburg, Germany only in 2013. As of 2016, it operates on four different continents and now receives hundreds of applications from all corners of the globe for every place offered on its training programmes.

These programmes train young people to take up pivotal environmental challenges, like how to deal with billions of plastic coffee cups discarded daily, and already reach young entrepreneurs and corporate executives in over 80 countries. Their university programmes for students committed to self-development, purpose and entrepreneurial skill are taught at some of the world's best universities, from Oxford to Columbia or Tsinghua University in China.

My teaching and lecturing work now brings me into direct contact with about 40,000 people annually, and with many hundreds of thousands through social media and TED talks. I observe that connections are now happening quickly between those who have already woken up to the changes happening in our world, and those waking — whether young social entrepreneurs, NGOs, or business people — because all have, to some extent, moved from 'me' to 'we'. They care less about how much they have and more about how much they can offer. They want to improve things for others, rather than impress.

These young social entrepreneurs in particular have discovered the secret: if the mantra of last century was "What can I get?" they know that the mantra of this century is "What can I give?" What they're willing to do is to risk all that others would guard so jealously — career, fame, wealth — to do what they can to make the world a better place. What's more, they love the adventure in this.

As more citizens begin to wake up to what's possible, we seem to be realising that the earth really is ours to protect and defend. And I am by no means the only one who sees this happening. Dr Monica Sharma, from her vantage point of years of experience at the United Nations, describes the new pathways being charted that are generating results — leaders reducing maternal mortality in parts of South Asia, transforming the lives of miners and neighbouring communities in the world's second largest platinum-mining company in Africa, involving artists to share their wisdom and create new approaches to violence at home and in society.

"These leaders are pattern-makers", she says, "not just problem-solvers. They deal with what is not working by creating alternatives. They are able to identify, distinguish, design and generate responses that integrate the different domains related to the entangled hierarchies of any given situation. They do not only solve complex societal problems at a surface level. They actively address the deeper dimensions."[129]

The rise of feminine intelligence in men and women

Perhaps more profound and far-reaching than any other current phenomena is the shift from a paternalistic 'top down' approach to change ("the leaders are in charge") to a laterally organised 'bottom up' series of initiatives springing up all over the globe. Some of those most reported are fundamentalist and authoritarian in orientation, but there is a significant and entirely unreported movement arising from a perspective of connectedness and responsibility for the future.

The motivation for this is the dawning realisation that there is no deity in the sky giving orders, but rather that humanity is interdependent — or as Desmond Tutu puts it: "I am, because you are". This is based on the discoveries of quantum physics but also from the experience that our lives work best when we take care of one another, when we allow ourselves to feel the suffering of others, and when we respect and support the abundant nature on which we depend.

This is the shift of attention from 'me' to 'we'. It makes use of the right hand side of the brain (inclusivity, intuition, creativity and the capacity to see the 'whole') as well as the left (rationality, logos, measurement, focus).

It also engages the energetic intelligence of the heart to work in combination with the mind. "The heart has a system of neurons that have both short- and long-term memory... The heart sends more information to the brain than the brain sends to the heart. Coherent heart rhythms help the brain in creativity and innovative problem-solving."[130]

This fundamental shift in how we perceive ourselves and the world has produced an extremely comprehensive array of initiatives and organisations, many of which have been described in detail elsewhere.[131] Those whose work I know from experience are Rising Women Rising World and FemmeQ.[132]

Rising Women Rising World is a vibrant community of women on all continents who take responsibility for building a world that works for ALL. This work is sourced from deep feminine wisdom and values, co-creating a vision of how the world could be in 2030, and proposing strategies to realise this, based on successful existing initiatives worldwide. Their global network, power of collaboration and strategic approach brings this work to fruition.[133]

The feminine intelligence that exists in both women and men is now needed to face the current crises and bring a radical shift in the way we live and lead. The masculine and feminine principles must be brought into balance. This is the fundamental understanding behind the launch of FemmeQ, namely that indispensable feminine wisdom and qualities are essential for human survival: the potency of compassion, the effectiveness of deep listening, the brilliance of intuition and the power of inclusivity. Marginalised for centuries, these qualities are emerging strongly again.[134]

Online activist networks

Avaaz is a global web movement to bring people-powered politics to decision-making. Launched in January 2007 it promotes global activism on issues such as climate change, human rights, corruption, poverty, and conflict. It is reputed to be growing at one million per month to become the globe's largest and most powerful online activist network with over 40 million members, claiming to unite practical idealists from around the world.

Other online activist networks are springing up daily, from the original models like Moveon.org to SumOfUs, 38 Degrees and many more. Many of these groups started out as online petition networks, which were not so long ago dismissed for encouraging lightweight and ineffectual 'clicktivism'. However they have now become crowd-funding powerhouses, enabling well resourced campaigns that impact corporate corruption, as well as educating responsibly on key issues.

Coeō is a geo-social network for conscious changemakers, connecting individuals and organisations at a local community level to enable collaboration and meaningful local action.

Through the geographical focus of the platform, users are encouraged to find other conscious, awakened individuals in their local area and, via the messaging tools provided, connect and form empowering, offline connections which in turn will enable collaboration and positive community action.

Coeō has brought together a unique and growing network of movements, creating much-needed unity. Thanks to Coeō, members from a growing number of groups such as Ubuntu Planet, The Full Circle Project, Prepare for Change, The Freedom Cell Network and The Conscious Media Coalition are coming together, connecting and collaborating. The local connections made between members of these varied groups is enabling greater collaborative action at a grassroots level.

On 26 November 2015 Avaaz published as follows: "ISIS's goal is to split the human family. To divide the world's 1.5 billion Muslims from everyone else... Muslims are almost one quarter of humanity, and 99 per cent are as horrified by the ISIS attacks as everyone else. They have been the greatest victims of ISIS, and have the greatest power to help defeat it. So let's answer hate with humanity, and seize this chance for transformative change. For all of us — Muslims and Non-Muslims everywhere — to fiercely welcome each other into our one human family like never before. ISIS attacks seek to spread hate and fear to divide the world's 1.5 billion Muslims from everyone else. Let's answer their hate with wisdom."

Daily, for those of us involved in social change, our inboxes are packed with evidence of people getting together, finding each other on-line, gaining confidence that what they believe in is "not weird but shared", and beginning to form alliances.

At present it might look to an outsider like a motley upsurge of new groups emerging with a vital energy and determination for change, but little cohesion.

However more cohesive plans emerge daily, with alliances forming to connect citizens across the planet, evolving very fast. What is emerging is that at local levels, at national and at global levels, increasing numbers of people from all walks of life are prepared to invest their time and skills in making the PREVENTION plan a reality. This next chapter shows how.

Global Coeō users, 14 Jan, 2017

Figures from Coeō

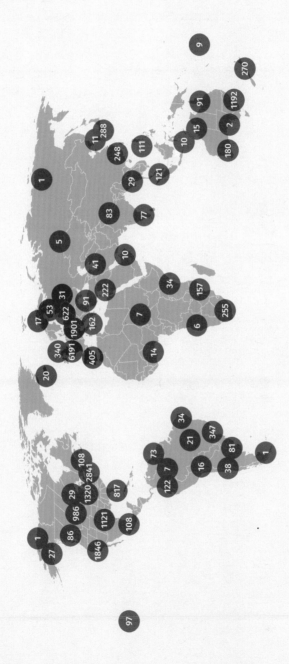

Chapter 7

Here's What You Can Do if You Want to be Active to Prevent Violence and Armed Conflict

Many of us — especially in this unsettled and divided political climate — feel a compulsion to "do something" but don't know how to set about it. This chapter offers all sorts of ideas and proposals showing how we can make a difference, even just using a few spare hours during a busy week. It is often easier to work in a group with friends, or to join something that already exists rather than to contemplate setting it up yourself, so on offer below are some things you can do on your own, and some that work best in a group.

Support non violence in schools and at home

Many schools are now finding that the simple steps of Non Violent Communication (NVC) work extremely well to minimise bullying and teach children skills that will be invaluable throughout their lives. So if you as parent or grand-parent want to propose NVC to your local school, you can find out how this works on the CNVC website.[135]

You can also break any cycle of violence in your own family or community, by opening dialogue and using Non Violent Communication. Take a two-day foundation training in NVC, it will change your life. It changed mine. It's common sense really, and not difficult: you can also use the Conflict Transformation Technique in the USEFUL TOOLS at the end of this book.

Boycott 'rich-lists' and celebrity rubbish; re-place with 'Local Hero Lists'

Having identified the local leaders you admire — women leaders, great teachers, responsible CEOs, people transforming society — then get hold of your local radio, and ask them to do a profile, featuring the value of this person's qualities — integrity, generosity, courage, creativity... Ask your local media to run a cumulative list of such heroes, so the local community can be aware of them and celebrate them at special events.

Systematically support locally-led peace initiatives

In every area where there is tension, you can bet there is some group who are trying to mediate between factions, bring down the temperature, get people to see the others' point of view. Find out who's doing this in your area. They may be quite low-profile.

Insight on Conflict tracks the kind of organisations you might like to support or volunteer with; just in Northern Ireland there are 19 initiatives! Have a look at www.insightonconflict.org/conflicts/northern-ireland. You can also check on the website of Peace Direct, who support a network of trusted and effective peace-builders in Africa and Asia, local heroes who are saving lives, helping people escape poverty and bringing hope to their communities.[136]

Address radicalisation through mothers

In the UK, mothers are beginning to take responsibility for their young sons and daughters at risk of going to Syria or Iraq to fight for ISIS or become jihadi brides. These young people are now being informed by some sheikhs on the internet that the Koran does not condone killing, and by contrast that "your jihad is with your mother".[137]

Gulalai Ismael, who works with young people 'at risk' in Pakistan and Afghanistan, asks people in safe countries to look on the website of Peace Direct[138] and decide which locally led initiative they want to support. She also urges them to hold their own governments accountable for supplying weapons to conflict areas.

In your school, community or workplace, make known the shock stats (then invite them to try some of the actions in this section)

- In the US in 2017, more people were shot and killed by toddlers than by terrorists.[139]
- Each day 16,000 children die of easily preventable causes. That is 750 an hour.[140]
- Producing 1kg of beef requires about 15,000 litres of water.
- Nearly half of humanity do not have internet access.
- Between 1992 and 2011, less than 10 per cent of those at the negotiating table — and only 4 per cent of those who signed peace agreements — were women.
- 65 million people are now refugees worldwide — a rapidly growing number — the highest ever.
- In the US, 6,500 former military personnel killed themselves in 2012. More veterans succumbed to suicide than were killed in Iraq.
- A world dominated by turbo-consumerism offers us no hope. It burns the planet.
- Oceans are acidifying at their fastest for 300 million years, which may precipitate collapse of the global eco-system.
- Runaway inequality has created a world where 8 men own as much as the poorest half of the world's population. And their wealth has fallen by a trillion dollars since 2010 — 38 per cent drop.[141]
- Between 100 and 200 entire species of creature are becoming extinct daily.
- 50 per cent of the world's wildlife and 50 per cent of the earth's trees have disappeared in just 200 years.
- Over 300,000 Indian farmers have committed suicide because they are forced to buy non-reproducing seeds. Since Monsanto's entry into India in 1998, the price of cotton seeds has increased by 71,000 per cent.
- If less than one per cent of the 15,000 nuclear weapons in the world were to explode, tons of debris would enter the stratosphere, lower the earth's temperature, destroy the stability of the ozone layer and end agriculture as we know it. In sum, a nuclear exchange of the arsenals of only India and Pakistan would end civilisation everywhere.[142]

"You are the last best hope of earth. We ask you to protect it. Or we, and all the things we cherish, are history."[143]— Leonardo DiCaprio

Support alliances of cities standing for peace values

If you live in a city, ask if your city is one of the United Nations Peace Messenger Cities. These are cities around the world that have volunteered for an initiative sponsored by the United Nations to promote peace and understanding between nations. The movement began in the International Year of Peace 1986, when 62 cities were chosen from among thousands. The International Association of Peace Messenger Cities was established in 1988 at Verdun, when representatives of these 62 cities met, to participate in the building of a world less violent and more humane, a world of tolerance and of mutual respect, to enable the requirements of peace based on justice and human rights to be better understood. Now, member cities meet twice a year with the aim of exchanging programmes, ideas and experience in cities around the globe.[144]

....

Join one of the Constellations in Rising Women Rising World (RWRW)

Through their Constellations, RWRW serve to build a vibrant community of women on all continents who take responsibility for pioneering a possible future. The custodians of this mission are a committed group of professionals, who over the past 30 years have been shaping their respective fields. We call these women Pioneers.

Each forms the nucleus of a Constellation — a further 12 women and men specialising in a particular field, be it education, environment, business, community, food & water, etc. They in turn train and mentor constellations of younger women and men to develop initiatives and projects that demonstrate how this kind of future world is not only possible, but is already happening.[145]

Replace stale values with interdependence values

There's plenty of evidence from left and right throughout Europe that citizens are tired of current political systems. They are fed up with corruption, with governments caving in to corporate pressures to weaken or destroy environmental laws; disgusted that the poorest half of the world population owns the same amount as a small group of the global super-rich.

To change this will take many new younger leaders, strong enough personally and politically to break out of the status quo, to build new political institutions, and to stand up for a totally new set of values based on interdependence. You'll have your own ideas as to what these values are, but if you need inspiration see the very last section of this book.

Start a campaign, like these students who triggered a massive divestment from fossil fuels

Started by a small group of university students in Philadelphia, "350" — named after the ppm amount of CO_2 in the atmosphere that still maintains climate safety — became a global grassroots climate movement that focused on holding leaders in various positions accountable to the realities of science and the principles of justice. Their argument was simple and twofold, supplementing a moral incentive with an economic one: it is not only wrong to profit from climate change, but it also is no longer a good investment as fossil fuel assets are losing value. The campaign inspired institutions to divest around 5.4 trillion from fossil fuels; another 5.2 billion was divested by individuals as of

January 2017.[141] The effects are becoming apparent: 13 US coal producers lost more than 92% of their value since 2011,[147] and in December 2016 Bloomberg News declared that "Solar power, for the first time, is becoming the cheapest form of new electricity."

....

Address the persistent and long-term influence and effects of trauma by making friends with refugees, with veterans suffering from PTSD, with war orphans

Barcelona seeks to welcome refugees and migrants into the fabric of the city, but its efforts have been stymied by the national government. Cities and activists across Europe are fighting their national governments to better welcome refugees.[148] If you enquire, you'll find there will be a centre for refugees and migrants somewhere not far away from where you live. They will direct you to children and adults who would welcome a friend. Help for Heroes will be able to inform about how to contact war veterans who might welcome a listening ear, and your respect for their experiences.

There are at least 16 ways you can support Syrian refugees now, by donating not just your money, but your spare time. Fear that refugees will take jobs, and lack of economic opportunities for refugees, make it hard for them to generate income. Combine this with the lengthy time it takes to process work visas for refugees and it can be hard for refugees to feed their families. This is part of what inspired #WorkforRefugees.[149]

....

Here's what you can do if you want to be active at national levels:

Campaign for your government to build a national Infrastructure for Peace

See the earlier section describing these in chapter 4. Most governments have never even thought about this. So make an appointment to see the person in your government who works closely with the prime minister or president. Say that you have a strategic plan to ensure safety and security throughout the country, at a very low cost. Copy the section in chapter 4, and discuss it with this adviser. In conclusion ask what form it should be presented in — and more importantly who it should be presented by — to be of maximum interest to your leader. Engage peace and women's organisations to support this Plan.

"Let's build a world in which we systematically train peace-builders in every part of the planet in the skills of Gandhi, Mandela and Aung San Suu Kyi, developing the kind of courses that combine the practical skills of peace building and non violence with the development of inner intelligence or self knowledge that can bridge the gap between 'us' and 'them'. Imagine if graduating from such a course became a basic qualification for standing for election to any public office!"

Organise massive global on-line support for politicians who take a stand

Leaders who take a stand on an issue often find themselves criticised and sometimes vilified. Opponents are usually noisier than supporters, and often personally unkind. If you support someone, make sure you let them know; write to them and ask what you can do to show your support. Why not help set up a global "Best List" for leaders like Angela Merkel (readers please add names) who stand up for innovative programmes that may be unpopular with conservative factions. Margot Wallström, the Swedish Minister for Foreign Affairs who prohibited Swedish arms exports to Saudi Arabia, was subjected to an organised campaign of vilification; she needed massive, open, loud support. Don't sit still when something you care about happens; it's so easy now to find out how best to show your support.

....

Point out to editors of your national media how frequently they carry stories about war and terror, compared to how rarely they feature the brilliant stories of peace-builders

"The clamour of war stories across screens, newspapers and airwaves perpetuates a great silence: the stories of ordinary people on the ground fighting for peace. Here in the U.S., our own country's brutal role as a major exporter of war is too often submerged, muting our connection — and accountability — for conflicts abroad."[150] — Peace is Loud

Feed them regularly with the extraordinary stories of unknown people who risk their lives daily so that others don't get killed. This acts as protection for peace-builders, because if they are known internationally, they are less likely to be attacked. For example, Peace Direct managed to get the BBC to make a documentary film and publish various newspaper articles about Henri Bura Ladyi.[151]

Henri Bura Ladyi regularly faces militants in the Congolese bush to undertake sensitive negotiations, the sort that only local actors can do because they are trusted by all parties. Henri and his colleagues have convinced 5,700 militia fighters to put down their weapons and leave the bush.[145]

Celebrate those who prevent armed conflict

Make them heroes, send them messages of support, send them small sums of money that they will use in incredible ways.[152] Examples of these heroes are the White Helmets: in Syria where public services no longer function, these unarmed volunteers risk their lives to dig people out of bombed buildings — regardless of their religion or politics. They have saved more than 60,000 lives — and this number is growing daily.[153]

Help train and reward teams to negotiate the safe removal of dictators

It's amazing what a few courageous and determined women can do.

Two civil wars in Liberia left 600,000 dead and hundreds of thousands of women raped and brutalised. Responding to the conflict, Leymah Gbowee mobilised an interreligious coalition of Christian and Muslim women and organised the Women of Liberia Mass Action for Peace movement. Through Leymah's leadership, thousands of women staged pray-ins and nonviolent protests demanding reconciliation and the resuscitation of high-level peace talks. The pressure pushed President Charles Taylor into exile, and smoothed the path for the election of Africa's first female head of state, fellow 2011 Nobel Laureate Ellen Johnson Sirleaf.[154]

If women leaders in other civil wars have the support of people worldwide, including training, capacity building and small amounts of money, they would be able to do what Lehmah and colleagues did. So when you read about a civil war, call the journalist and ask for the names and contacts of the women resisting it.

Join 'Beautiful Rising'

August 2016 saw the launch of a new activist toolkit, Beautiful Rising,[155] aimed at helping people put an end to injustices like militarism and dictatorship. Comprised of community organisers, trainers, tech gurus and writers across six continents, the Beautiful Rising team is working to broaden the relatively thin library of resources on creative non violence and social change strategy. What's more, they've done it in a way that takes into consideration the concerns of activists in the global south: security, accessibility and usability.

Their advisory network helped the team roll out regional collaborative workshops over the past two years in Myanmar, Bangladesh, Mexico, Zimbabwe, Uganda and Jordan, where content for the toolkit was gathered and pocket versions of the *Beautiful Trouble* book were distributed.

....

Contact and support indigenous groups; learn from their wisdom

The insights of indigenous peoples are based on very ancient beliefs and practices that can help to overcome our inherited belligerence and our apathy, to develop a different attitude to our role on this planet. Their values based on love and respect for the planet and all living elements on it have been clearly articulated recently by indigenous leaders in the US. There are a multitude of examples.

The Eagle and the Condor story of the Amazon people is an ancient prophesy in which human society splits into two paths: The path of the Eagle, based in logic, the industrial, and the sacred masculine; and the path of the Condor, based in heart, intuition, and the sacred feminine. The story says that after a 500-year period in which the Eagle people dominate the Earth, the Eagle and the Condor people will come together to create a new level of consciousness for humanity.[156]

Help shift military activity away from preparations for war towards crisis response

Building on previous research, the Oxford Research Group concludes that the main security issues of concern in the future are likely to arise from climate change, economic inequality, migration and competition over resources, and that none of these is suited to a conventional armed response.

For young people concerned about the future security of their country, it therefore makes more sense to direct their energies to working in NGOs, international organisations or ministries that seriously address global warming, environmental protection, the rich-poor gap, refugee and migrant issues and exploitation of natural resources.

Young people who consider a future career in the military could, at interview, stress their wish that military activity shift away from the primary role of preparations for war towards more conflict prevention, crisis response, cooperative international action, etc. The reality of soldiering, as returning veterans will attest, is very different from the glamorous advertisements. As already mentioned, in the US, 6,500 former military personnel killed themselves in 2012. More veterans succumbed to suicide than were killed in Iraq. In 2013, the United States Department of Veterans Affairs released a study that covered suicides from 1999 to 2010, which showed that roughly 22 veterans were committing suicide per day, or one every 65 minutes.[157]

Draw up a list of qualified women to fill policy-making roles on peace & security in your country

First, take a look at how many women hold senior positions in your ministry of foreign affairs, defence or development. If this is less than 50/50, then draw up your own list of women you see to be qualified and able to bring a conflict prevention perspective to the tasks of that department. Talk to your national women's organisations and get their suggestions, and their backing to send the list to the relevant ministers. If you get a meaningless response or no response at all, contact your national media.

Engage with PEACE IS LOUD [158] who spotlight women leaders on the frontline of peace-building worldwide. They "harness the power of film and other media to bring to life the leadership of everyday people who are standing up to violence and building peace from the ground up". They organise speaking engagements and other live events spotlighting women peace-builders from Afghanistan to Zimbabwe whose courage and activism are altering the history of nations. They create social action campaigns that encourage and empower people to build peace in their day-to-day lives — in their own communities and as citizens of the world.

Support The Life You Can Save: ending extreme poverty this year

The Life You Can Save[159] is adamant about the fact that extreme poverty can be solved. And it did drop from 43 per cent in the eighties to 9.5 per cent in 2015. This leaves 702 million people that struggle to survive on the equivalent of US $1.90 per day, adjusted for local buying power.[160] The organisation estimates it would take 28 billion a year to meet the most basic health and nutritional requirements of the world's neediest people, providing education, sanitation and healthcare for all.

RE-vamp national budgets for prevention of conflict

By calling your ministry of foreign affairs or defence, find out how much your government spends on the prevention of conflict; you may need to be very specific in your enquiry, as there is usually a global figure attributed to 'conflict resolution'. Ask what the prevention budget is and what it is spent on.

Make suggestions as to what further funds could be spent on, with greater effectiveness. One such suggestion would be to contribute to a local or regional Rapid Response Fund, as described in chapter 4.

Build a ring of iron around PMs and advisers

Today's leaders are besieged by lobbyists who put enormous pressure on them to act in ways that favour commercial interests. Some of the pressures they exert are actually threats. So before your new leaders come into office after election, help pull together a group of tough, trustworthy advisers who can protect them from unnecessary interviews with pressure groups and corporate leaders. This thinking is similar to what inspired the formation of The Elders...

"This group [The Elders] can speak freely and boldly, working both publicly and behind the scenes. Together they will support courage where there is fear, foster agreement where there is conflict and inspire hope where there is despair."[161] — Nelson Mandela

Join a group of emerging female leaders who are shifting values

For example, reject the concept of "growthism". A world dominated by turbo-consumerism offers us no hope. It both burns the planet and stretches social solidarity to breaking point. We have to do better than the offer of:
* things you didn't know you needed,
* bought with money you don't have,
* to impress people you don't know.

The politics of love, time, creativity and care must come first.

....

Support leaders who take responsibility for past actions

For example, Canadian PM Justin Trudeau apologised for an 102-year-old slight to Indians, mainly Sikhs.[162] "As far as I am concerned, the ability to acknowledge a wrong that has been done, to simply say sorry, will go a far, far, far longer way than some percentage of GDP in the form of aid," MP Tharoor.[163]

....

Here's what you can do if you want to be active at international levels

"It is impossible to accurately portray the devastating effects that global challenges will have on us all unless unified global action is taken. Our shared challenges call for global solutions, and these solutions will require cooperation on a global scale unparalleled in human history."[164] — Steve Killelea

Often it can feel daunting to intervene at international levels, but increasingly change is happening by the sheer pressure of the opinion of millions of people. So now is the time to gain confidence in what any individual can do, even by simply adding their weight to others...

Ensure that the company you work for becomes a 'B Corps'

B Corps are for-profit companies certified by the nonprofit B Lab to meet rigorous standards of social and environmental performance, accountability, and transparency. Today there is a growing community of more than 1,600 Certified B Corps from 42 countries and over 120 industries working together toward one unifying goal: to redefine success in business. If your employer is not yet part of this network, gather a group of employees to propose it to your Board. Look up www.bcorporation.net/what-are-b-corps

Change legislation on tariffs and trade barriers

Joseph Stiglitz has suggested several solutions for a fair trade regime; "solutions must be pro-poor and pro-development". For example "Rich countries should simply open up their markets to poorer ones, without reciprocity and without economic or political conditionality. Middle-income countries should open up their markets to the least developed countries, and should be allowed to extend preferences to one another without extending them to the rich countries, so that they need not fear that imports from those countries might kill their nascent industries."[165]

Secondly, eliminate subsidies in 'the West': "Since the vast majority of those living in developing countries depend directly or indirectly on agriculture for their livelihood, eliminating subsidies and opening agricultural markets would, by raising prices, be of enormous benefit", but as not all developing countries would benefit (eg farmers would benefit but importers would suffer as prices rise), industrial countries should "provide assistance to help developing countries through the adjustment period — even a fraction of what they now spend on agricultural subsidies would do."[166]

....

Clean up oceans

Terry, Christina, and Chris are friends who read about the Great Pacific garbage patch (a vast semi-dissolved island of waste twice the size of France), were disgusted, and invented a simple solution: the SeaVax, a solar-powered ship that can suck up to 22 million kgs of plastic a year. Just a small number of these ships would clean up the entire Pacific garbage patch in just 10 years.[167] Imagine a major multi-national getting behind such a popular initiative...

....

Is your country one of the ten countries at the top of the Global Peace Index?

If (in 2017) you live in Iceland, Denmark, Austria, New Zealand, Portugal, Czech Republic, Switzerland, Canada, Japan or Slovenia,[168] your government has discovered the advantages of investing in a peaceful society. Thus you can take the initiative to persuade your leaders of the advantages of investing in one of the ten least peaceful countries in the world, supporting the leaders of that country. You would open a dialogue with your business leaders to assist with investment in that country, to inspire projects to multiply employment opportunities.

As we now know, young men are drawn to trafficking because there are no jobs. In Egypt half of young people live below the poverty line. Your business experience and sense of entrepreneurship would help provide employment in a country afflicted by conflict, and that would do a great deal to stop not only armed violence, but also economic migration. Media coverage would also help to change the current narrative of fear, which makes people feel hopeless and constantly anxious.

....

Help organise a youth campaign for a 2.5 per cent tax on the global arms trade

In 2014, at least $94.5 billion worth of arms sales were agreed on, of which two-thirds were to developing countries. The five permanent members of the UN Security Council together with Germany and Spain account for over 80 per cent of the arms sold between 2010 and 2014.[169]

A 2.5 per cent tax levied on current annual arms sales would yield approximately $2,360,000,000. This revenue could be invested in addressing the root causes of conflict, including the proposals formulated above.

So you, as an ordinary citizen, could propose a campaign to one of the massive popular movements like Avaaz. Avaaz are 100 per cent funded and guided by their community. Every campaign run is first polled and tested to a random sample of that community; if there is a negative reaction the team goes back to the drawing board and comes up with a better option. 100 per cent of Avaaz funding comes from small online donations and any donations from corporations, governments, foundations, and even individual donations over 5,000 Euros are refused.

....

Join campaigns against your country trading weapons

In June 2016 the British High Court ruled that The Campaign Against the Arms Trade can take the government's decision to keep arming Saudi Arabia to a judicial review. The High Court ruled, on the 10th of July 2017, that the UK's sales of arms were "lawful." Reports say: "The judges said "closed material", which had not been made public for national security reasons, "provides valuable additional support for the conclusion that the decisions taken by the secretary of state not to suspend or cancel arms sales to Saudi Arabia were rational".[170] You can ask your MP to sign EDM 136 — a parliamentary petition calling for an end to arms sales to Saudi Arabia.

On 7 September 2016 the UK parliamentary Committees on Arms Export Controls issued a draft report saying the UK should stop selling arms to Saudi Arabia while Saudi actions in neighbouring Yemen are investigated; and that it was highly likely that weapons had been used to violate international humanitarian and human rights laws. Two days previously Foreign Secretary Boris Johnson defended the selling of arms to Saudi Arabia for potential use in Yemen, insisting the export of weapons to the country would continue.

Dr Samantha Nutt, doctor and founder of War Child, suggests a bold, common sense solution for ending the cycle of violence. "War is ours," she says. "We buy it, sell it, spread it and wage it. We are therefore not powerless to solve it." She recommends insisting that your government ratify the Arms Trade Treaty. As of May 2017, 89 states have ratified or acceded to the Treaty, including five of the world's top 10 arms producers (the United Kingdom, France, Germany, Italy, and Spain; but not China, Russia or the USA). You can look up and see if your country has signed and ratified.[171]

Join one of the new social and political movements

The social and political movements that have unfolded across Europe in the last five years, like Podemos and Nuit Debout, have yet to be connected to the representative elements of democracy in any sustained or substantive fashion. The 'Brexit moment' may create space for the kind of radical regeneration of progressive politics that may be possible in times of crisis. New political institutions need new people to make them work, especially leaders who can break out of the status quo and create space for others to follow suit until some sort of tipping point is reached.[172]

DiEM25 is fostering a network of rebel cities, from Barcelona and Valencia to Napoli and municipalities in Germany and Poland. As they say in their Manifesto:

"While the fight for democracy from below (at the local, regional or national levels) is necessary, it is nevertheless insufficient if it is conducted without an internationalist strategy toward a pan-European coalition for democratising Europe. European democrats must come together first, forge a common agenda, and then find ways of connecting it with local communities and at the regional and national level."[173]

Join a Non Violent Peace Force

Nonviolent Peaceforce is an unarmed, paid civilian protection force that fosters dialogue among parties in conflict and provides a protective presence for threatened civilians. They have developed ways of mobilising the capacities of local communities in Sri Lanka, and now extend this methodology to South Sudan. You can train with them to use your western status to give added safety to local peace activists by accompanying them.

Nonviolent Peaceforce has been nominated for the 2016 Nobel Peace Prize by the American Friends Service Committee: "Unarmed civilian protection is a method for direct protection of civilians and violence reduction that has grown in practice and recognition. In the last few years, it has especially proven its effectiveness to protect women and girls" according to a UN report of October 2015.

....

Support 'Simultaneous Policy'

This is a truly brilliant idea: the Simultaneous Policy (Simpol) is a range of citizen-designed policies to bring about economic justice, environmental security and world peace. It is also a movement of world citizens who use their votes to drive their governments to implement those policies — simultaneously. With simultaneous implementation, no nation suffers any competitive disadvantage so all nations win. This means politicians risk nothing if they support Simpol. When citizens join the campaign, they give strong preference at national elections to politicians who have signed a pledge to implement Simpol, to the probable exclusion of those who haven't. As support grows, politicians who fail to support Simpol will increasingly lose their seats to those who do.[174]

....

Get behind the Astana Vision

On 29 August 2016, at an international conference co-hosted by the Parliament of the Republic of Kazakhstan, Parliamentarians for Nuclear Disarmament and Non-Proliferation from many countries agreed The Astana Vision: From a Radioactive Haze to a Nuclear-Weapon-Free World — a 10-point action plan for nuclear disarmament.[175] You can present this practical 10-point plan to your own member of parliament and ask them to present it to their party leader.

....

This is simply a snapshot of the initiatives we are aware of so far. You will have so many ideas and experiences of your own, so we hope soon to have a website where you can add them to our list of what any individual — particularly those in safe countries — can do to support people at risk of their lives in unsafe countries.

Chapter 8

The Qualities of People Doing This

This chapter is a change of pace. On first glance it's about the qualities of the people involving themselves in preventing violence, whether at home in the community or in an area of armed conflict. At a deeper level it's about becoming awake to what's going on, becoming aware of the skills we need to use, and developing the presence to use them. It's an opportunity to:

- go further into these skills of self knowledge
- examine how best to take a stand
- learn how to work with inner conflict
- clarify what it is you want to contribute to your community or the wider world

"I am as much concerned with the human condition in general as with specific conflicts, which often represent only the tip of a pyramid of violence and anguish... In this sense the social worker, the teacher, the wise legislator, or the good neighbour is just as much a peacemaker as the woman or man un-ravelling some lethal international imbroglio."
— Adam Curle

Why is this important? In half a century of work in the world, the most important lesson I've learned is that inner work is a prerequisite for outer effectiveness, for the simple reason that the quality of our awareness directly affects the quality of results produced. The story of Chris Hughes at the start of this book is a striking example — his awareness and presence of mind saved many lives that day in 2003.

The new brand of leaders that we need — those who are actually able to meet the challenges of today and thrive in the world of tomorrow — are the ones who know and live the connection between inner self-development and outer action. If we want to communicate clearly, transform conflicts, generate energy, and develop trust within our families and in our places of work, our first challenge is to do the inner work.

This is the current evolutionary challenge that most people don't yet grasp: that the desired outer changes cannot come about without the inner change. If a critical mass of humanity can make this shift, an entirely new way of living can emerge. The challenge is for an evolutionary shift, a leap in our ability to move from thinking about 'me' to thinking about 'we'.

This may seem difficult at first, but soon it becomes clear that it is a nourishing and satisfying way to live, because what human beings are drawn to is a sense of purpose in life, and what many of us search for in our lives is a feeling of belonging, a feeling of community.

In short, we have to do deeply personal work to be less personal!

When I was 30 I contracted a brain disease that put me in a coma for two weeks and took six years to recover from. During this period my brain was too foggy to attempt any kind of research, but there was just one thought that went round and round in my head. It was: "Who am I?" "Who am I?" Eventually I found my way to a person who could help with what was then an unusual enquiry, and gave me some tools to start answering this question.

Over many decades I have found that the capacity for self-awareness and insight is essential in those who are working to prevent or resolve conflict. The greater the level of self-awareness you have, the less your unresolved personal issues will taint your actions and the greater the effectiveness of the work you do. For example, it is clearly essential for those mediating between opponents not to be driven by anger or fear, but to have already recognised and addressed their own darker emotions.

When it comes to political issues, many of us get caught in a cycle of selfrighteousness or blame that keeps us politically stuck — an attitude that can obliterate any prospect of real dialogue with those holding other views.

While working on nuclear weapons I became acquainted on intimate terms with my own self-righteousness — the captivating, invigorating notion that I am right and 'they' are wrong. The moral high ground is not a good place to be... neither useful nor effective. I have realised painfully over the years that if I genuinely want to open a dialogue with someone, I have to be open to accept what he is communicating to me, and to even consider the awful possibility that I might be wrong.

The other danger, found among many in the media, is to get stuck in cynicism. To be cynical is actually painful and joyless; it stops opportunities flowering before they are even in bud, and it can turn us from flesh to stone.

Upgrading our awareness is incredibly exciting, because it means we become alert to far more of what's going on around us, instead of being self-obsessed. It means seeing beauty in our lives, intense pleasure in the present moment, and possibility in our future.

Aung San Suu Kyi (above) is Foreign Minister and Leader of the National League for Democracy in Burma. Before her party won a landslide victory in 2015, she was under house arrest for the greater part of 15 years. "Freedom for her is not just a set of institutions, laws and political processes, it is also a quest ... for the development of self awareness that turns us from victims of our emotions into their masters. Self awareness, she believes, allows us to control emotions such as greed, fear and hatred; if we increase our mastery of these feelings, it will lead to a 'revolution of the spirit', which will inform and transform the conduct of politics."

Given the frightening news on our TV screens daily, many people become apathetic. Helplessness makes people feel lost. For many of us, that indicates the need to change our own inner landscape — away from "I'm not good enough" or "there's nothing I can do" — and moving towards "how can I help?" or "what can I give?"

By gaining this perspective you are able to respond rather than simply reacting to events. You may feel fear, but you can choose not to react from fear, but instead from a more secure place.

So now we shall look at some of the ways of doing this.

The ability to feel your emotions

It is essential to feel what you're feeling, and most of us have learned not to do this, because it's often felt to be 'too much'. However, if we avoid examining our feelings they are then repressed, can retreat into the unconscious and can suddenly re-emerge and ambush us.

By allowing yourself to simply stay very still 'with' an emotion, holding it quietly in your heart, you will find that it will transform — all by itself. This may sound unlikely, and you will only know the truth of it when you try it. When you have developed self-awareness — meaning the ability to understand your emotions so that they don't rule you — you can gain the 'inner space' to be able to take an honest look at yourself.

Let's be clear: we are not talking about controlling impulses, because that simply becomes another function of the mind. We are interested in deeply feeling the feelings, so that we get to know them well, and are no longer afraid of the strength of them.

Empathy is the great blessing inherent in this — it's the ability to identify with and understand the wants, needs, and viewpoints of those around you. John Paul Lederach, one of the most insightful and experienced of peace-builders, calls this 'dynamic curiosity'. He says that communities who managed to break the historical grip of violence were "never quite content with facile views and answers, they kept searching to better understand the conflict, themselves and 'the other'".[176]

People who know and understand their own feelings are better at recognising the feelings of others. This means they avoid stereotyping and judging too quickly, and tend to live their lives in a very open, honest way. They can manage disputes, are excellent communicators, and are masters at building and maintaining relationships.

In Useful Tools at the end of this book you'll find a delightful page on "10 Tips for Effective Communication" by Liz Kingsnorth, who's a real expert.

The ability to listen

More conflicts are prevented or resolved by having the ability to listen, than by any other means. Most of us think we are good listeners, and most of us are not. When we are apparently listening, we spend most of our time thinking what we're going to say next, or judging the other person, or interpreting — or simply not being present.

Your full undivided attention is the greatest gift you can give another person, especially in an argument. A person who feels truly heard starts to relax. Better still, if the listener is concentrating hard enough to begin to hear the emotions behind the actual words, all sorts of information emerges. Crucially, the interaction can move from the head ("I'm right and you're wrong") to the heart ("Oh my goodness... is THAT how you feel?").

Let me give an example. Working with the global executives of a major international company recently, I asked them to undertake an exercise sitting in pairs opposite one another for 40 minutes. They were required to keep eye contact, and listen intently while their partner answered questions like: "What's disturbing you in your life?" "What are you yearning for?" "What's your highest potential?" Each partner took a turn answering, by going well below the cognitive to the gut level, and each took a turn listening, which meant giving absolute attention.
At first they hated it. Bodies squirmed with the embarrassment of eye contact and personal honesty. But by the end they had a new take on the power of listening, and after using it at work for a few weeks, the CEO reported: "What you taught us enables us to resolve in 15 minutes what would previously have taken four hours of argument, and still not been solved."

So if you want to be able to practise your listening skills, and see just how good a listener you are, try the Listening Exercise in the USEFUL TOOLS section at the end of the book.

Mindfulness

I am certain that a different future for all of humanity is possible, if leaders wake up. Interestingly, this is happening quite swiftly now in the corporate world. Making a contribution, mindfulness and inner work are now seen as essential tools in many leading companies, extensively featured in the Financial Times and on the cover of Time Magazine.

However, waking up means more than sitting quietly in meditation. It means going deeper into self knowledge, into the value of integrating the wounded parts of yourself. It will hopefully guide you to discover something you have been blind to about yourself, the "gem under your dragon's foot". Waking up also means learning to take a stand on issues that matter to you, and the importance of time spent alone to decide how you can be most useful.

Getting to know your shadow
— the value of integrating the wounded parts of yourself

Every one of us has a shadow, which can consist of things that happened when we were young, deep hurts and past experiences that may be largely unconscious. If they remain unconscious they can trigger unexpected behaviour. For example, I found myself enraged by a colleague when we were co-leading a workshop, and became so incensed that the entire group could feel a sense of unease. When I looked into it, I realised that my anger was caused by my feelings of jealousy for what she was saying, wanting to be the centre of attention myself! This came from childhood experiences when I had felt overshadowed and overlooked by four big strong brothers who could do most things better or faster than I could! When I realised this and took care of those feelings, the anger vanished.

This kind of self knowledge can only be acquired by a process of honest self questioning. We can do this by noticing when we get triggered, by someone else, and taking time to look into our feelings in a kindly gentle way.

It also involves getting to know our Inner Critic. Mine makes me lose my sense of self. I can become a jelly in a few minutes, by simply allowing my critical voice to mutter at me. My confidence drains out, as though my soles had holes. And most of us have an Inner Critic — in fact even the most successful executives and top civil servants admit that they suffer from "impostor syndrome", meaning that they feel that sooner or later they'll be caught out as a fraud!

One way to deal with a bothersome Inner Critic who keeps insisting that you're "not good enough" is to have a dialogue with your demon. To find out how to do this, see the Inner Critic Exercise in the USEFUL TOOLS at the end.

If you choose to enter dialogue with someone in a decision-making position, be aware that this may spark some feelings of inferiority in you — the "they know best" syndrome, referred to in an earlier chapter.

Gather a Tribe

When we undertake challenging work to change and transform current issues, it can be a very lonely business. And lonely fighters make mistakes; I have been there and I know. So what we need is to gather around us a TRIBE — people who hold a compatible vision of how the future could be, people who know how to support and nourish one another, how to listen deeply when things go wrong and not try to 'fix', people who hold a strong space for change, people with whom to celebrate.

As you move into self awareness, at the same time as honing what it is you want to contribute to the world, you will notice people along the way who are on the same path. If they are possible kindred spirits, gather them. Check out if you place the same value on transparency, open-ness, internal growth; also see if it's fun to be around them. Those are good signs for the beginning of your tribe.

Taking a stand

If you are part of the system or 'establishment' — or if you are not and would like them to take your views on board — then it can be hard to tell the unpalatable truth. If you do, it is often perceived as trouble-making — which means you become marked out as 'not one of us', which means you don't get invited to in-crowd events, which means that no-one even hears what you have got to say.

But if you don't tell the truth, your betray yourself and possibly the future of your company or organisation, or your family for that matter. Quite a trap, for all concerned — a trap for the establishment because if the truth is never told, decisions progressively deteriorate and the emperor ends up going around without his clothes.

In the 1980s and 1990s I frequently felt like Daniel in the lion's den. Once I was invited to the Royal United Services Institute, Britain's main military think tank, to give a lecture on secrecy and accountability in British defence decision-making. I was led into the ancient library where 55 men (and one woman) from the Ministry of Defence and the Foreign Office were sitting (one of the Institute members told me that not many years ago a woman appeared at one of these meetings and a senior military officer remarked loudly "There's a woman. Who is she? Is she somebody's wife?").

I had decided to talk about nuclear weapons, and how little Parliament knew about the facts — who's in charge of decisions, who they are targeted at and even how many we have. We are not told when there is an accident that might cause cancer in those working on the warheads. And so on.

Then came question time. I knew from experience that these things are like a gladiatorial contest. After the main gladiator has shown himself off, the others stand up and show themselves off in trying to hack him down. So the way you answer the first question is key to how much blood the rest of the room will smell. An aggressive man asked the first question in the "You're not seriously suggesting that …?" mode. I was taken aback by the sarcasm but I thought a bit of ju-jitsu might work, and asked him how he would answer his own question. He opened and shut his mouth several times, and we passed on to a more genuine tone of seeking improvements to the system.

Therefore it is worth preparing yourself well for this work, so that in mind, body and spirit you are well able to be fully present whenever the moment demands. In your mind you need to be very clear about what you think, the points you want to make, and the tone you will take. Any kind of aggression must be replaced by your own integrity, because integrity has a palpable energy.

Nelson Mandela has quite a raspy voice, and does not do oratorical flourishes, but when he started to speak to a preliminary meeting of The Elders, I got goose bumps. When he finished speaking 35 minutes later, I still had them. I asked myself "what is this?" Some time later I realised that what I was experiencing was energetic; I was getting nothing less than the energy of his integrity.

You will want to take care of how your body helps you present yourself. Instead of crossed legs or arms, take a sturdy stance with your feet really feeling the ground or, if you are sitting, sit as if on a throne. Take some moments beforehand to exercise your voice with deep clear tones, and above all, breathe very deeply and consciously throughout. The reason for this is that oxygen will then get to your brain which, to say the least, will be helpful to enable your points to flow smoothly.

Your spirit will be the key to your effectiveness, and will need just as much exercise and nourishment as your mind and body. Make sure you spend time regularly in self reflection. In my experience — for my own clarity — it's essential to have a daily practice of quiet contemplation. It can be meditation, walking in nature, chanting, whatever you choose, but make sure it's regular. Why? Because quietness is when good ideas can drop sweetly into your consciousness. Quietness is when you learn things about yourself and others that you didn't know. Quietness gives you grounding, and grace.

A little contemplation is even useful in meetings. You don't believe me? When we had the first Chinese delegation of nuclear decision-makers come to Oxford, we organised a public meeting in St Anthony's College, which I chaired. At one point the disagreement between Chinese and British officials was becoming tense — voices were raised and the translators couldn't keep up. So I said "Now we shall take a few minutes just to absorb what has been said, to digest it and let it settle. So we shall have silence for three minutes." Somewhat to my astonishment, everyone complied. Or pretended to.

With the current widespread uptake of mindfulness, many high performing teams in corporate, artistic and sports arenas regularly have short periods of silence at the beginning of — or during — meetings.

Time alone

When decisions need to be made, or when I need nourishment, I spend time on my own. I miss my sense of self when I am too much with other people, and I need to listen to still small voices within.

Once when I had been at an intense conference in a grand setting I found I had missed my sense of grounding for those two days of talk and food and wine. I only got it back after it was all over and I went for a walk. I saw a sign saying "Cow Pond". Not at all a pond, it was more of a great mysterious lake surrounded by ancient oaks, murmuring slightly — the kind of hidden place that makes adults sigh, and children go quiet and begin to daydream. It was covered in great pink and red water lilies. Frogs hopped up onto their leaves. The afternoon was hot and dappled and busy with bees. I could sink down on the bank and rest my mind and muse, leaving the intellectual exercise of the previous days behind.

Beauty has that effect on people — it allows us to ground ourselves and get beyond the ego. Or at least be a little less driven by it.

Deciding how you can be most useful

So many people today are asking: " I see all these problems surrounding us, but what can I do?"

The first question to ask yourself is: "What breaks my heart?" because this is where your passion will be. It will arise in whatever matters to you most, be it cruelty to children, the plight of refugees, torture, or the abuse of women...

So observe what goes on in you when you watch TV, listen to the news or read the papers. When you feel your heart beating faster, that means your empathy is engaged and you're on track for where you can best contribute.

The next step is to think calmly about your skills. What are you really good at? Are you a good communicator, do you like organising, or are you good at social media, or doing budgets and accounts? Do you have a few hours you can spare to draw friends together around an issue?

Then marry the two. Connect your passion with what you're good at. For example, If you live in a city, ask if your city is one of the United Nations Peace Messenger Cities and gather a group of friends to support that. Or if you really care about how female genital cutting disables millions of girls and women, and you happen to speak good French and love doing social media, you could find out easily who is doing the best work on FGC in West Africa, ask them what they need and volunteer your services. You will almost always need to volunteer for at least six months before the outfit you want to work with can see where you can really be useful, and even then you may need to raise the funds so that you get paid.

Unless you have a lot of experience, I would not recommend that you start your own organisation, because the whole business of registration (as not-for-profit or charity) will take much of your energy, and raising funds from scratch is a major challenge when you don't have a track record.

Getting practical — turning your dream into action

In the section previously entitled "Deciding how you can be most useful" you learned how to connect your passion with what you're good at.

Now we can look at practical steps. The first step is to get set up and sustainable. You may find you can join an existing organisation that has the same passion and the same aims as you. This will give you vital experience.

Then there may come a time when you have very specific goals, and you need to spell them out as clearly as you can, and how you see a plan to achieve them. At that point do please research if anyone else is already doing what you want to do, and if there is, go talk to them, because it's always better to join forces.

Partnering is vital in this time of ferocious change, when currently very sparse resources are devoted to the prevention and resolution of conflict. Talk through with your potential partner what it is that you have the skills to do, what you want to achieve, and find out what would dovetail or augment what they are already doing.

Your next challenge is to build an aligned team — harnessing the energy of a conscious group. You will surely make a very conscious choice of people to include in the team, making sure they have done the inner work referred to above. My experience has taught me not to take on anyone who is not interested in inner work, because it makes transparency in an organisation so much quicker and easier. At interview I would recommend asking questions about self awareness and 'being willing to walk towards conflict'.

You would also want to be clear you are aligned around shared purpose. Some people are pure visionaries — absolutely lyrical and passionate about ideals — but are inspirational rather than practical and incapable of getting anything actually done!

It's also a great sign when people are willing to admit what they don't know. Key to the good functioning of a team is Transparent Communication — if you can share the values of open-ness, admitting mistakes, saying what's really going on — this can be the essential glue for a team. In the USEFUL TOOLS you'll find a page that may well be helpful, entitled Holding meetings that energise: building trust to permit transparent communication.

So here are the essentials for your journey: emotional intelligence, the ability to listen, getting to know your shadow, taking a stand, having time alone, deciding how you can be most useful, working with conflict, and getting practical — turning your dream into action. And how thrilling it will be to see you turn your dream into action!

Your achievement

Did you know that according to the research by the Barrett Values Centre on the hierarchy of qualities of a 21st-century leader, the highest level of consciousness, way above self esteem or even 'making a difference', is service? Barrett describes it as "selfless service in pursuit of your passion, purpose or vision".[176]

This is also the experience of the most effective peace-builders worldwide. They know that the inner power you develop — the self knowledge and awareness of your own strengths and your own demons — is vital to the effectiveness of anything you undertake. I would go so far as to say this inner power is essential, because it will enable you

- to firmly take a stand when you need to
- to manage disappointment when something goes wrong
- to observe yourself 'projecting' your unresolved emotions onto others
- to feel energised, fulfilled and joyful as you live your life

In this way you will become robust as well as empathic, courageous as well as sensitive, resilient at the same time as being full of grace. In short, you will become a noble person, in service to your community and the world.

"Yearning has a way of making us more willing to start a personal meditation practice, and it illuminates the need to make conscious choices in daily life to support such a commitment. The paradox is that we must stop, feel, and grow silent in order to receive the gift of ourselves even while we still hang on to the belief that things are all up to us, that we are in charge."[178]

Working with conflict — the gem under the dragon's foot

Inevitably, in any initiative to bring new ideas to the world, there will be conflict. And you can use the energy of conflict. It does not have to be prevented or resolved, but transformed.

Most of us avoid conflict, because it's so uncomfortable. But conflict doesn't disappear just because it's dismissed! It simply festers, and then breaks out suddenly when you're under stress. So the best possible thing you can do is to walk towards tension and discomfort, rather than running away or dodging it. Walking towards it means finding the right moment to say to the other person or people, "I feel we have some tension here between us. Would you be willing to talk about it in a safe, calm way?"

Ask them if they would be willing to sit with you for half an hour and talk in a structured way. Explain that this will give both parties an opportunity to express feelings safely, rather than going into the rights and wrongs of the situation.

Then use the conflict transformation technique in USEFUL TOOLS. What this process does is to move
- from the head (being 'right' and having a 'position')
- to the heart (being connected) where you suddenly start to get what it is like to be the other person

This means you can move from your opposing 'positions' round to a place where you can both look at the problem from a perspective of your 'interests' — what you both need. If all goes reasonably well, you're moving towards a place of communication, a softening of what was previously hard and harsh.

Developing this skill is one of the best things you can do in your life — for your family, your relationships, and your service to the planet.

And the payoff is, when you have the courage to walk towards the conflict, to face the dragon that is breathing fire, you will discover some truth about yourself, and possibly the other person will too — some truth that you never knew. We call this 'the gem under the dragon's foot'.

Conclusion

I hope that the journey taken through this book — from the analysis of the drivers of war right through to this celebration of individual potential — will help you, my reader, to take your own steps. You may not realise how profoundly you are needed in the world today, and how the world longs for you to be of service. We are going through such fundamental changes, changes that may be un-nerving and frightening, but which are the necessary disruptive precursors to a new stage in the evolution of humanity. We are being invited to be part of a leap in human consciousness, a shift that will enable us to act as balanced, empathic, whole people capable of working together for the benefit of us all.

The most powerful and lasting way to counter war and violence is to build a culture of peace. Peace is more than the absence of war. Peace means living together with, and even celebrating, our differences — be they cultural, political, religious, ethnic, racial or gender-based. Peace involves transforming society from the inside out, in our own lives and across borders. A culture of peace rests on a strong foundation of respect for justice, dignity and human rights that can now spread exponentially with your help.

USEFUL TOOLS

This Toolbox provides answers to the question of "How do I do this?" and contains trusted exercises to develop some of the skills that you will probably need. These tools have been well tested for efficacy and practicality in different cultures, and I trust that they will serve you well.

Tips for Effective Communication

Liz Kingsnorth[179] explores the ways we can improve our relationships with others at home, at work and with friends, with 10 suggestions on how to improve the way we communicate.

1. An intention for connection

Aim for a respectful and compassionate quality of connection, so that everyone can express themselves, be heard and understood. Trust that the connection is more important and more nourishing than being right, or even just having your say. Connection means to try to be open and stay in touch with what matters to the other person — and to yourself — in each present moment.

2. Listen more than you speak

We have two ears and one mouth — a reminder of what is important! Listening is key to a healthy relationship. Often we are only half listening, waiting for our chance to speak, wanting to make our point. When our attention is with our own thoughts, we are not listening. Listening means to enter into the world of the other person, to intend to understand them, even if we disagree with what they are saying.

3. UNDERSTAND THE OTHER PERSON FIRST

When another person feels you understand them, they are far more likely to be open to understanding you. Willingness to understand involves generosity, respect, self-control, compassion and patience. Be 'curious instead of furious' about how others are different from you.

4. UNDERSTAND NEEDS, WISHES AND VALUES

Everything people say and do expresses an underlying need, longing or value. We can learn to identify and 'hear' these needs, even when they are not expressed explicitly. Because all human beings share these needs, they are our magic key to unlocking mutual understanding. For example, if someone says, "You are so selfish, you never do anything to help at home," they are indirectly expressing a longing for consideration and support, but it is coming out as blame and judgment. If we can empathise rather than react, we will connect and the person will feel understood.

5. BEGIN WITH EMPATHY

Refrain from:
- Immediately telling your own similar story
- Interrogating with lots of data-type questions
- Interpreting the other's experience
- Giving advice
- One-upping, e.g. "if you think that's bad wait till you hear about what happened to me!"
- Dismissing the person's feelings, e.g. "Oh don't be angry."
- Dismissing the person's experience, or telling the person that this experience is actually good for them!

Generally people appreciate receiving empathy more than anything else.

6. TAKE RESPONSIBILITY FOR YOUR FEELINGS

What someone else says or does is not the cause of how we feel, it is the trigger. Our feelings are stimulated by what's happening. For example, if someone does not do what they say they will do, we might tell them, "You make me so angry, you are so unreliable!" This inflammatory accusation could be rephrased as, "I feel frustrated because it's important to me that we keep to agreements we have made."

7. MAKE REQUESTS THAT ARE PRACTICAL, SPECIFIC AND POSITIVE

Make requests that will help fulfil our needs. This stops us just complaining, and allows the situation to change. Don't ask things of others that are too vague or too big, or are expressed as a negative request, e.g. "Stop making so much noise." Be positive and specific, e.g. "I am working. Can you please use the headphones while playing video games?"

8. USE ACCURATE, NEUTRAL DESCRIPTIONS

When we are upset, we often interpret what has happened, using judgmental language, rather than accurately describing what has triggered us. This can get us into a fight immediately! For example, instead of simply stating, "You didn't call me," (which is a fact) we often interpret this wrongly and make an accusation, like: "You don't care about me!" So it's best to first describe the situation in a neutral, accurate way, free of judgments or blame. Then the communication can continue with sharing feelings, needs and requests. For example, instead of saying, "That's a really stupid idea!" you might say, "If we all go to a movie which ends at midnight [neutral description], I'm worried [feeling], because the children need to get a full night's sleep [need]. Can we go to the 2 p.m. show instead [specific request]?"

9. Be willing to hear "No"

Even with these guidelines, our carefully expressed requests might still elicit a "No" from the other person. Why would this upset us? Is it that our request was actually a demand that we expect the other person to fulfil? We have a choice in how we hear that "No". It could be that something else is important to the other person; that they had a different need or value alive in that moment. Maybe the "No" is their request for something else to happen. And then we are into the dance of giving and bending! "No" is not as threatening as we might imagine.

10. Ways we communicate other than words

Everything that is in our heart and mind is expressed through our body, our facial expressions, the tone of our voice, and the vibrations that emanate from us. All these are intuitively picked up and understood by others. Are our words in harmony with these subtler elements? We are manifesting our conscious-ness at every moment. To have connection, understanding and harmony in our relationships, we need to nourish those aspects deeply within ourselves.

The listening exercise

This exercise has four benefits:
- A profound deepening of your understanding of what's really going on inside you and another person
- Discovering the authentic self from deep within — what you didn't know you knew
- Checking your ability to give another person your full attention without 'helping'
- It reveals compassion and opens the heart

I've done this exercise with corporate leaders, top executive teams, and young social entrepreneurs from all over the world. They all found it quite tough to do at first, but came out of it astonished at what they found — their own truths as well as others'. You can also do it with your lover or partner; if you've hit a sticky patch it's an incredible way of getting past the blame game and learning what's happening inside yourself and inside your partner.

It's important to agree absolute confidentiality, because you may be saying or hearing things that are extremely private, tender and vulnerable — things that may never have been said before.

Sit down opposite each other somewhere comfortable where you won't be disturbed for twenty minutes, with a timer. One partner is **A** and one is **B**. Agree on a non-trivial question, for example "tell me who you really are?" or "tell me what you long for most in your life?" Set the timer for 5 minutes.

Partner **A** asks the question thus: " Tell me [name of partner] who you really are?" then does nothing else except to give full listening attention. That means keeping eye contact but not reacting — not nodding, smiling, laughing or grimacing. This isn't exactly easy, but essential because when we 'encourage' another person — or react in any way —we subtly affect what they decide to say.

Partner **B** undertakes the following sequence:
1. Gives their full attention to the question
2. Puts their full intention on finding out the truth of the answer
3. Takes the question down from the brain into the belly
(the 'hara' or centre of gravity of the body)
4. Reports whatever answer is there

It's important for Partner **B** to report only what is there — not give all the back story — and then do the technique again for the 5-minute period. The more honestly you can report what is there, be it embarrassing, shameful, astonishing or funny, the more you will discover.

So Partner **B** may not say a great deal before going silent again while re-peating the 4-part sequence over a period of 5 minutes. Meanwhile Partner **A** simply continues to give full attention and does not repeat the question.

After 5 minutes the timer will ping, and you change over. Partner **B** asks partner **A** the same question and then follows the same instruction to simply give full attention and eye contact. Partner **A** undertakes the sequence 1—4 above.

You can do just one question, which will take about 10 minutes, or you can go on and do 4 questions of your choice, which will take about 40 minutes.

Other questions people sometimes use are:
- Tell me [name of partner] what's disturbing you in your life?
- Tell me [name of partner] what are you yearning for?
- Tell me [name of partner] what unlocks your heart?
- Tell me [name of partner] what gives you energy?

When you finish you can decide if you want to simply write in your journal, or share feedback. You'll be amazed what you find out about yourself, your listening skills, and about what really matters to your friend.

The INNER CRITIC exercise

Within everyone there are critical forces within us that can crush our imagination and cripple our energy, can shrivel our ideas and reduce us to helplessness, can take us away from who we truly are. These are the forces we wish to understand and transmute. The Inner Critic gets traction in the following ways:
- You have a major challenge coming up, and doubt of your abilities takes over
- You are suddenly ambushed by an incident in your past, perhaps where someone made you look foolish
- A carping voice sits on your shoulder saying: "You don't belong." "You're not good enough to do this." "You're not loved." "You're a fraud."

The attitude of the inner critic can sabotage us at any time, so it's worth working on. The origin of it almost always lies in early experiences of humiliation or shame or rejection. It is painful to trace these, but necessary. When these are 'presenced' and felt in a supportive space — with a trusted friend perhaps — these feelings can complete themselves and dissolve, and then the Inner Critic will inevitably carry much less energy. You can follow these steps:

1. Please recall when you said to yourself one of the above phrases, or similar. Write down the incident(s) that caused the Inner Critic to get traction, and at what age.

2. Look back at the situation and observe the difference between the facts of the incident and the meaning you made of it. Notice how the meaning you made of it can pull you away from the very things you're committed to.

There is also a useful exercise to do on your own to transform the Inner Critic: So, when it next wakes you in the middle of the night:

- Breathe deeply and calmly for a few minutes
- Set out two cushions or chairs
- Sit in one, and speak to your Inner Critic as if it was sitting opposite
- Ask it why it is bothering you. Ask "What do you want of me ?"
- Then get up and actually go and sit in the Inner Critic's chair, and answer as if you are the Inner Critic. It may feel a little strange but you will find that if you give it a chance, it will speak very clearly. It will probably surprise you.
- Go back to your own chair or cushion, and take in what it has said. Ponder it. If you have a further question, like "Why do you want me to do this ?" or "What do you know that I don't know ?" then ask it.
- Then go across to the Critic's place, and answer again, in the Critic's voice. It will have an unusual wisdom.
- Continue the process until you have heard and digested what it says.
- Then see if you can agree a plan with the Critic, one that answers its need, and one that is comfortable and possible for you to carry out.
- Carry out the plan.

It works. You'll see.

Holding meetings that energise: building trust to permit transparent communication

Ask employees of any large company or organisation and they will complain that they spend too much time in boring meetings. This frustrates and de-energises people — feeling that they waste time feeling uninvolved and impatient. So the art of holding meetings that energise is well worth learning. Here are some ground rules that produce more fruitful meetings and help to build trust in the team. For example, introduce a culture where you agree to:

- Start meetings with a few moments of silence to allow everyone to 'arrive' — not just physically but for the heart & mind to be present, leaving distractions behind;
- Hold a 'check-in' where each person says briefly how they are in that moment or expresses any concerns or expectations of the meeting; (it needs to be understood that there are no 'negative' emotions and no emotion that needs 'fixing'. Just heard/received.)
- Agree total confidentiality if appropriate;
- Agree when the meeting will end, and stick to this;
- Listen while another is talking and not interrupt (a talking stick is useful);
- Talk without raising the voice or using accusing language;
- Appoint two facilitators, one responsible for process and one for content:

The process facilitator monitors the quality and focus of the meeting by periodically 'taking the temperature' of the meeting, stating if there appears to be anger in the air, for example, or sadness; sometimes asking people to share briefly how they are feeling at this present moment; if necessary calling for a brief pause — an agreed silence to allow everyone to settle and 'collect themselves' and digest what has been said. It's good to both start and end the meeting with a 'check-in' and 'check-out', when each person can say a sentence or two about how they're doing. This builds trust, and enables participants to become aware of the emotional state of their fellow stakeholders. The content facilitator keeps the conversation on topic —

- pointing out when it is going off;
- periodically summing up 'where we've got to';
- ensuring the agenda items are covered in the time available; making sure at the end of meeting everyone is clear about next steps.

It's essential to practise these skills, because establishing trust between mutually suspicious parties who may have caused each other harm is not easy. That's why we use the word "holding" a meeting: the facilitators are literally "holding the space" in which transformative results can be developed. To build resilient trust between stakeholders one has to go beyond concerns of physical or psychological security. Very often exposing vulnerability or a trace of humanity can be the doorway to building deeper trust. An example:

One of the key inspirational moments of reconciliation in South Africa was when Nelson Mandela took a helicopter to have a cup of tea with Bessie Verwoerd, widow of former President Henrik Verwoerd — the grand architect of apartheid. For many this encounter was unthinkable. It had an incredible impact on Afrikaner extremists — that the man they were trying to portray as a danger-ous criminal had the trust and integrity to pay a civilised visit and have a cup of tea with someone who would have been his sworn enemy.

Transforming 'power-over' to 'power-with'

As mentioned at the end of chapter three, a key aspect of the prevention of violence lies in an understanding of power. Power-over others is the use of bullying, domination, physical strength and ultimately military force. By contrast power-with others is co-operative, creative, and depends on nothing other than the integrity of an individual.

This exercise will enable you to gain a better understanding of how power-over (domination power) and power-with (inner power) work through you.

1. Recall a situation where you used domination power or power-over to master a situation. Write down your answer to the following questions:
- How did it make you feel emotionally and physically?
- Was this way of proceeding necessary?
- What were the short and long-term effects?

2. Now consider a situation where someone used domination power over you and answer the following questions:
- How did it make you feel emotionally and physically?
- As far as you can see, was this way of proceeding necessary?
- What were the short and long-term effects?

3. Now think of a situation in which you used power-with or inner power to act in a situation, and reflect on these same questions.

4. To conclude, imagine the situation in step one and consider what would have happened if you had used inner power. Envision yourself standing there, recall the particulars of the situation and the urgency with which initiative had to be taken. Feel yourself receptive to others and wiling to cooperate while remaining grounded in your integrity.
- How does this make you feel emotionally and physically?
- Do you see new possibilities to act in the situation?

Conflict transformation technique

... but there may be a diamond underneath its foot. The wisest sages say that this is the very reason why it is worth your courage to actually meet the dragon of your conflict. So here's what to do:

Ask the person with whom you have a conflict if they would be willing to sit with you for half an hour and talk in a structured way. Explain that this will give both parties an opportunity to express feelings safely, rather than going into the rights and wrongs of the situation.

Two people involved **[A & B]** sit opposite each other, preferably with a neutral facilitator, and preferably with some flowers nearby (this helps to ground us and remind us that beauty still exists, even in a conflict).

1. **A** starts to describe his/her feelings in the conflict, speaking in the first person and not accusing **B**, for example "When 'x' happens, I feel — sad, angry, frustrated, miserable, fearful, etc..."

2. **A** continues until has said enough. **B** simply gives full attention and listens, does not interrupt.

3. **B** is asked to feed back to **A** what **B** has heard, as accurately as possible, plus what s/he has observed of the feelings behind the words.

4. **A** is asked "Was that correct? Was anything omitted?" **A** can then add anything that was left out.

5. Change over, and do the same with **B** speaking and **A** listening, etc, through steps 1 — 4.

During this process the facilitator can coach **A** or **B** to be more specific, to stick to the first person, to express feelings clearly, to be more authentic.

6. Then facilitator can ask **A** to express his/her NEEDS: "What do you need?" while **B** listens to the answer.

7. Then the same question to **B**, while **A** listens.

8. Then move to REQUESTS. Facilitator asks **A** "What do you request **B** to do/not do?" **B** can agree or not, and they can set a time frame if necessary, by which time **B** will do what **A** requests.

9. Same for **B**, to make a request of **A**. **A** to agree or not, and set a time frame if necessary, by which time **A** will do this.

This exercise is based on the concepts of Non Violent Communication, developed by Marshall Rosenberg, www.wikipedia.org/wiki/Nonviolent_ Communication.

To repeat, what this process does is to shift the issue from the head (basically "I'm right and you're wrong") to the heart, where you suddenly start to get what it is like to be the other person. This means you can move from your opposing 'positions' round to a place where you both look at the problem from a perspective of your 'interests' — what you both need. If all goes reasonably well, you're moving towards a place of communication, a softening of what was previously hard and harsh.

On reflection I feel that this exercise may be the most useful tool in the book.

NOTES

1.   The full story is told by Dan Baum, *'Battle Lessons: What the Generals Don't Know,'* New Yorker, 17 January, 2005. http://www.newyorker.com/magazine/2005/01/17/battle-lessons

2.   https://www.hrw.org/world-report/2017/country-chapters/syria

3.   https://www.unicef.org.uk/donate/syria/?gclid=CP3ufmhw9QCFdeRG-wodMRQHGA&sissr=1

4.   Calculated by the Institute for Economics and Peace, whose method is a comprehensive accounting exercise to 'add up' those direct and indirect expenditures related to creating and containing violence plus its consequential costs. These include not just military spending but domestic expenditures on security and police plus the losses from armed conflict, homicides, violent crime and sexual assault.

5.   *War costs us $13.6 trillion. So why do we spend so little on peace?* Camilla Schippa, World Economic Forum, 8 June 2016. https://www.weforum.org/agenda/2016/06/the-world-continues-to-spend-enormous-amounts-on-violence-and-little-on-building-peace/

6.   Diagram from 'Global Peace Index' 2016. http://reliefweb.int/sites/reliefweb.int/files/resources/GPI%202016%20Highlights.pdf

7. *Audit Reveals the Pentagon Doesn't Know Where $6.5 Trillion Dollars Has Gone*, Jay Syrmopoulos, Global Research, 16 August, 2016. http://www.globalresearch.ca/pentagon-cannot-account-for-6-5-trillion-dollars/5541244

8. http://worldbeyondwar.org/need-2-trillionyear-things-detail

9. *'Climate change seen as top global threat'*, J. Carle, 2015. Washington DC: Pew Research Centre.

10. http://europe.newsweek.com/climate-change-will-cause-worlds-next-migration-crisis-333024; September 2015.

11. http://europe.newsweek.com/climate-change-will-cause-worlds-next-migration-crisis-333024; September 2015.

12. The United Nations Water Development Report 2016. http://unesdoc.unesco.org/images/0024/002440/244041e.pdf

13. http://www.wri.org/blog/2015/08/ranking-world%E2%80%99s-most-water-stressed-countries-2040; August 2015.

14. https://www.oxfam.org/sites/www.oxfam.org/files/file_attachments/bp-economy-for-99-percent-160117-en.pdf

15. https://www.theguardian.com/environment/2002/aug/22/worldsummit2002.earth4

16. *Making Globalisation Work*, Joseph Stiglitz (2006), p.62.

17. *A Thousand Sisters*, Lisa Shannon, Seal Press, CA, 2010.

18. 'Soldiers Who Rape, Commanders Who Condone', *Sexual Violence and Military Reform in the Democratic Republic of Congo*, Human Rights Watch, 2009.

19. *The War on Women*, Sue Lloyd-Roberts, Simon and Schuster UK Ltd, 2016, p.148.

20. Dr David Hammond, Senior Research Fellow at the Institute for Economics and Peace. A copy of the 2015 Global Peace Index report is available to download, http://economicsandpeace.org/wp-content/uploads/2016/06/GPI-2016-Report_2.pdf

21. https://sustainablesecurity.org/2016/09/22/the-coming-peace-africas-declining-conflicts/

22. http://www.unitar.org/pmcp

23. http://www.osce.org/secretariat/conflict-prevention

24. https://www.sipri.org/databases/milex

25. Education for All Global Monitoring Report — UNESCO http://unesdoc.unesco.org/images/0023/002321/232197E.pdf

26. Clean Water and Sanitation: why it matters. http://www.un.org/sustainabledevelopment/wp-content/uploads/2016/08/6_Why-it-Matters_Sanitation_2p.pdf

27. https://www.sipri.org/databases/milex

28. *The Shadow World: Inside the Global Arms Trade*, Andrew Feinstein, Penguin, London, 2012, p.xxii.

29. http://www.sustainablesecurity.org/2016/08/24/markets-minerals-and-mayhem-in-darfur/

30. Richard Jolly, chairman of the Water Supply and Sanitation Collaborative Council, sponsored by the W.H.O.

31. http://www.gov.uk/government/uploads/system/uploads/attachment_data/file/541330/20160727_-_Official_Statistics_-_UKTI_DSO_Core_Slides_for_2015_-_Final_Version.pdf

32. *'Bombs fall from the sky day and night': Civilians under fire in northern Yemen'*, London: Amnesty International, 2015.

33. In this sector I am relying on the paper by the Ammerdown Group, *Rethinking Security: A discussion paper*, Ammerdown Group (2016), p.11. https://rethinkingsecurity.org.uk/rethinking-security-a-discussion-paper/

34. *'National security strategy and strategic defence and security review 2015: A secure and prosperous United Kingdom'*, London: Cabinet Office, 2015, p.20 & p.77.

35. Statistics collated by UK Trade and Investment, a government body that promotes British exports abroad.

36. 'Two-thirds of UK weapons have been sold to Middle Eastern countries since 2010.' http://www.independent.co.uk/news/uk/home-news/britain-is-now-the-second-biggest-arms-dealer-in-the-world-a7225351.html

37. https://www.nytimes.com/2015/04/19/world/middleeast/sale-of-us-arms-fuels-the-wars-of-arab-states.html?mcubz=1

38. Speaking at the Vatican, 12 May 2015, Pope Francis condemned both the arms industry and those who profit off war, the Catholic Herald reported.

39. http://www.cfr.org/peace-conflict-and-human-rights/sunni-shia-divide/p33176#!/

40. *Rethinking Security: A discussion paper,* Ammerdown Group (2016), p.11. See Note 28.

41. Adapted from *Rethinking Security: A discussion paper*, p.39.

42. 'Women's Participation in Peace Negotiations: Connections between Presence and Influence,' United Nations Entity for Gender Equality and the Empowerment of Women, available at http://reliefweb.int/sites/relief-web.int/files/resources/03AWomenPeaceNeg.pdf

43. 'Beyond Victimhood: Women's Peace-building in Sudan, Congo, and Uganda,' International Crisis Group, June 28, 2006.

44. Statistical analysis by Laurel Stone, as featured in O'Reilly, Ó Súilleabháin, and Paffenholz, 'Reimagining Peacemaking,' 12–13. http://www.inclusive-peace.org/sites/default/files/IPI-Reimagining-Peacemaking.pdf

45. Jacquleine O'Neill, 30 December 2016.

46. *'The national security strategy of the United Kingdom: Security in an interdependent world'*, London: Cabinet Office. MoD, 1998. *'Strategic Defence Review'*, London: Ministry of Defence. *'A Strong Britain in an Age of Uncertainty: The National Security Strategy'*, London, HM Gov., 2010. *'National security strategy and strategic defence and security review 2015: A secure and prosperous United Kingdom'*, London, HM Gov, 2015. All courtesy of Ammerdown Group (2016), *Rethinking Security: A discussion paper*, p.11. See Note 28.

47. http://www.iraqinquiry.org.uk

48. Adapted from *Chilcot: all peaceful options were not exhausted,* by Gabrielle Rifkind and Scilla Elworthy, 15 July 2016, https://www.opendemocracy.net/uk/gabrielle-rifkind-scilla-elworthy/chilcot-all-peaceful-options-were-not-exhausted

49. http://www.alternet.org/story/149393/Wikileaks per cent27_most terrifying_revelation per cent3A_just_how_much_our government_lies

50. *Rethinking Security: A discussion paper*, Ammerdown Group (2016), p.8. See Note 28.

51. 'Military to military', Hersch, S. M., *London Review of Books*, 7 January 2016.

52. *Rethinking Security: A discussion paper,* Ammerdown Group (2016), p. 12.

53. Ibid p.14.

54. *'Tribe – on homecoming and belonging'*, Sebastian Unger, Hachette, New York, 2016, p.48.

55. Adapted from *Rethinking Security: A discussion paper*, Ammerdown Group (2016), p.23. See Note 28.

56. http://www.dalailama.com/messages/world-peace/the-reality-of-war

57. Rifkind op cit, jacket cover.

58. Now made into a documentary film by Danish director Peter Anthony, *The Man Who Saved the World*.

59. Personal communication from Dr Mo Mowlam, May 11 2004.

60. Conciliation Resources, work in review, 2009.

61. 'Mighty be our powers', Lehmah Gbowee, p.174.

62. *'Understand to Prevent: The military contribution to the prevention of violent conflict'*, Multinational Capability Development Campaign, 2014.

63. 'US Military Oil Pains,' Suhbet Karbuz, *Energy Bulletin*, 17 February, 2007, detailing the oil consumption just for the Pentagon's aircraft, ships, ground vehicles, and facilities that made it the single largest oil consumer in the world.

64. *Answer to Job*, C.G. Jung, CW 11, p.459

65. *Preventing violent conflict*, Department for International Development (DfID), 2006, p.4.

66. *War Prevention Works*, Oxford Research Group, 2001.

67. http://www.insightonconflict.org/about/

68. Conciliation Resources is an independent international organisation working with people in conflict to prevent violence, resolve conflicts and promote peaceful societies. http://www.c-r.org

69. International Alert has been working for 30 years with people directly affected by conflict to find peaceful solutions. http://www.international-al-alert.org/who-we-are

70. http://www.globalactionpw.org

71. Search for Common Ground partner with people around the world to ignite shared solutions to destructive conflicts. https://www.sfcg.org/what-we-do/

72. http://www.peacedirect.org/uk/pakistani-peacebuilder-gulalai-ismail-in-
    terviewed-bbc

73. http://www.youtube.com/watch?v=v5ZXDCV8wQU

74. 'Advancing Peace & Mitigating Crises — Recommendations and Proposed
    Language for the Foreign Assistance Act (FAA)', Concept paper from the
    3D Security Initiative and the Alliance for Peace-building, New York, 2010.

75. For a diagram of how this works see *Making Terrorism History*, by Scilla
    Elworthy and Gabrielle Rifkind, Rider, 2016, p.44.

76. Op cit, p.74.

77. https://www.peacedirect.org/child-soldiers/

78. http://www.buildingbridgesforpeace.org/about-building-bridges-for-
    peace/jo-berry-founder/

79. http://traumapro.net

80. See Working Paper of GPPAC on Infrastructures for Peace, http://www.
    gppac.net/news-and-media

81. 'Nepal, Ministry of Peace and Reconstruction: a foundation for Peace',
    Manish Thapa, *Joint Action for Prevention: Civil Society and Government
    Cooperation on Conflict Prevention and Peace-building*, GPPAC Issue
    paper 4, pp.55-61.

82. http://www.inclusivesecurity.org/about-us/

83. *Countering Extremism: Unconventional Wisdom and Uncomfortable
    Truths*, report from The Women's Alliance For Security Leadership (WASL).

84. Adapted from http://www.opendemocracy.net/5050/rahila-gupta/roja-
    va-revolution-it-s-raining-women

85. *A Road Unforeseen: Women Fight the Islamic State*, Meredith Tax, Belle-
    vue Literary Press, August 2016.

86. *Jihad – a British Story* has been nominated for a BAFTA.

87. http://www.theforgivenessproject.com/stories/desmond-tutu-south-africa/

88. http://www.politics.co.uk/comment-analysis/2015/07/08/comment-want-to-boost-the-economy-george-try-slashing-the-ar

89. http://www.workersclimateaction.files.wordpress.com/2009/07/lucas-briefing.pdf

90. *'Arms to renewables: Work for the future'*, London: Campaign Against Arms Trade, 2014. https://www.caat.org.uk/campaigns/arms-to-renewables/arms-to-renewables-background-briefing.pdf

91. *Move the Nuclear Weapons Money – a handbook for civil society and legislators*, IPB, PNND and WFC, 2016.

92. http://www.jeremyleggett.net/2016/07/state-of-the-transition-june-2016-a-long-list-of-advances-the-short-list-of-setbacks-including-brexit/

93. http://www.atkearney.com/sustainability/featured-article/-/asset_publisher/BqWAk3NLsZIU/content/the-profitable-shift-to-green-energy/10192#sthash.LsiQ0lTf.dpuf

94. https://www.theguardian.com/global-development-professionals-network/2015/sep/15/five-developing-countries-ditching-fossil-fuels-china-india-costa-rica-afghanistan-albania, September 2015

95. https://www.theguardian.com/world/2017/jan/05/costa-rica-renewable-energy-oil-cars

96. *Understand to Prevent*, see Note 57. http://www.gov.uk/government/uploads/system/uploads/attachment_data/file/518378/20150223-MCDC_U2P_Summary_Secured.pdf

97. *The Fog of Peace*, Gabrielle Rifkind and Giandomenico Picco, I.B.Tauris, London 2014.

98. *Developing a United Nations Emergency Peace Service: Meeting Our Responsibilities to Prevent and Protect*, H. Peter Langille, New York, Palgrave, 2015.

99. Such as a project of the university of Sydney Centre for Peace & Conflict Studies, with Caritas Australia and Global Action to Prevent War, New York. http://sydney.edu.au/arts/peace_conflict/images/content/uneps/uneps_brochure1.pdf

100. http://www.globalsolutions.org/files/public/documents/UNEPS_CGS_One-Step-Towards-Effective-Genocide-Prevention.pdf

101. *Alternatives to military intervention: a commando team of mediators*, Gabrielle Rifkind, openDemocracy 25 September 2014.

102. Philip McKibbin, 15 December 2015, https://www.opendemocracy.net/transformation/philip-mckibbin/hijacked-emotions-fighting-terrorism-with-love

103. https://www.theguardian.com/commentisfree/2015/nov/16/isis-bombs-hostage-syria-islamic-state-paris-attacks

104. *'Exposure – Jihad: A British Story'*, aired on Monday 15 June at 10:40pm on ITV1.

105. *Rethinking Security: A discussion paper,* Ammerdown Group (2016), p.68. See Note 28.

106. According to the latest regional economic outlook of the International Monetary Fund and http://gulfnews.com/business/economy/middle-east-s-youth-unemployment-expected-to-surge-in-coming-years-1.1620712.

107. http://www.sinaldovale.org/about-us

108. http://www.soundvision.com/article/a-call-for-shia-sunni-dialog

109. Ibid

110. Including the Muslim Women's Collective, Women Unify, Muslim Women's Network, Wise Muslim Women, the Muslim Women's Council, etc

111. http://www.acleddata.com/

112. http://www.ushmm.org/confront-genocide/how-to-prevent-genocide/early-warning-project

113. Women of Liberia Mass Action for Peace

114. http://www.international-alert.org/publications

115. Bhutan's Constitution: http://www.bhutanaudit.gov.bt/

116. http://www.ted.com/talks/tshering_tobgay_this_country_isn_t_just_carbon_neutral_it_s_carbon_negative

117. *Measuring Peacebuilding Cost-Effectiveness* published by the Institute for Economics and Peace, March 2017.

118. https://www.un.org/development/desa/publications/world-population-prospects-the-2017-revision.html

119. http://www.rt.com 11 November 2016

120. http://www.nytimes.com/2015/03/03/science/earth/study-links-syria-conflict-to-drought-caused-by-climate-change.html

121. http://www.citizensforsyria.org/mapping-syrian-cs/simplesearch/

122. Personal interview, February 2015.

123. http://www.wilpf.org/five-things-you-need-to-know-about-syrian-womens-grassroots-organisation-in-the-context-of-the-talks-on-syria/

124. http://www.peacedirect.org/uk/fight-or-flight-the-difficulties-young-people-face-in-somalia/

125. http://www.huffingtonpost.com/rabbi-shmuly-yanklowitz/syria-no-fly-zone_b_8223916.html

126. Andy Carl, Executive Director, Conciliation Resources.

127. Darshita Gillies, TEDx on 'Millennial Power' https://www.youtube.com/watch?v=c9fhYm4yMtk

128. http://www.thedoschool.org

129. 'Future Systemic Transformation: Leadership for Paradigm Shifts in an Interdependent World,' Monica Sharma, paper for The Emerging Future: Women Co-creating a World that Works, Oxford, UK, 28 October–1 November , 2013.

130. Research by the Heartmath Institute: Neurocardiology: Anatomical and Functional Principles, J. Andrew Armour, M.D., Ph.D., http://store.heart-math.org/e-books/neurocardiology

131. *Pioneering the Possible: Awakened Leadership for a World that Works*, North Atlantic Books, 2014, chapters 5 and 6.

132. http://www.femmeq.org

133. http://www.risingwomenrisingworld.com

134. http://www.femmeq.org

135. http://www.cnvc.org

136. http://www.peacedirect.org/uk/peacebuilders/

137. BBC Radio 4 — The Web Sheikh and the Muslim Mums

138. http://www.peacedirect.org

139. https://www.theguardian.com/commentisfree/2017/feb/08/trump-muslim-terrorists-gun-violence-america-deaths

140. UN Inter-agency Group for Child Mortality Estimation

141. https://www.oxfam.org/en/pressroom/pressreleases/2017-01-16/just-8-men-own-same-wealth-half-world

142. Global Security Institute, 16 December 2016.

143. http://www.youtube.com/watch?v=F47RIF_0reA&app=desktop

144. http://www.iapmc.org

145. http://www.risingwomenrisingworld.com

146. http://www.gofossilfree.org/commitments/

147. http://ieefa.org/market-cap-u-s-coal-companies-continues-fall/

148. https://www.opendemocracy.net/mediterranean-journeys-in-hope/buer-bner-hansen-cameron-thibos/welcoming-refugees-despite-state

149. See also http://www.globalcitizen.org/en/content/how-to-help-syrian-refugees-5th-anniversary-crisis/

150. http://www.peaceisloud.org/what-we-do/

151. http://www.peacedirect.org/uk/video-interview-henri/

152. You can find them on http://www.insightonconflict.org

153. http://www.whitehelmets.org

154. Documenting these efforts in the Tribeca Film Festival 2008 Best Documentary winner *Pray the Devil Back to Hell*, Leymah demonstrated the power of social cohesion and relationship-building in the face of political unrest and social turmoil.

155. http://www.opendemocracy.net/transformation/phil-wilmot/new-activist-toolkit-arrives-in-beautiful-fashion

156. *See How Indigenous Wisdom Can Inform the Global Transformation We Need,* December 7th, 2015 | By Jocelyn Mercado. http://www.pachamama.org/blog/how-indigenous-wisdom-can-inform-the-global-transformation-we-need

157. February 1, 2013. U.S. military veteran suicides rise, one dies every 65 minutes. Reuters.

158. http://www.peaceisloud.org/what-we-do/

159. http://www.thelifeyoucansave.org/Learn-More

160. World Bank, 2016. http://www.worldbank.org/en/news/press-release/2015/10/04/world-bank-forecasts-global-poverty-to-fall-below-10-for-first-time-major-hurdles-remain-in-goal-to-end-poverty-by-2030

161. http://www.theelders.org/article/nelson-mandela-introduces-elders-johannesburg-18-july-2007

162. http://www.timesofindia.indiatimes.com/nri/us-canada-news/Canadian-PM-Justin-Trudeau-to-apologize-for-102-year-old-slight-to-Indians-mainly-Sikhs/articleshow/51788038.cms

163. http://www.telegraph.co.uk/news/worldnews/asia/india/11762311/Indias-prime-minister-endorses-call-for-Britain-to-pay-reparations-for-colonial-rule.html, July 2015.

164. Steve Killelea, founder of the Institute for Economics and Peace.

165. *Making Globalisation Work* by Joseph Stiglitz, 2006, p.83

166. Ibid, p.87

167. http://www.ecowatch.com/2016/02/19/seavax-vacuum-ocean-plastic/

168. http://www.static.visionofhumanity.org/sites/default/files/GPI%20
     2016%20Report_2.pdf. p.8.

169. http://www.sipri.org/yearbook/2015

170. http://www.bbc.co.uk/news/uk-40553741

171. https://www.un.org/disarmament/convarms/att/

172. http://www.opendemocracy.net/transformation/michael-edwards/is-
     there-any-hope-for-new-age-politics

173. http://www.opendemocracy.net/can-europe-make-it/yanis-varou-
     fakis-rosemary-bechler-alex-sakalis-anthony-barnet/democratising-eu-
     rop

174. 'The Simpol Solution', John Bunzl and Nick Duffell, publ. Peter Owen Ltd,
     2017.

175. http://www.astanaconf2016.org/en/declaration/

176. *The Poetic Unfolding of the Human Spirit*, Fetzer Institute, 2011, p.5.

177. *'The New Leadership Paradigm'*, Richard Barrett, 2010, chapter 4.

178. Liz Kingsnorth, syndicated from http://www.heartfulnessmagazine.com,
     20 August, 2016.

Useful references

Nonviolent Communication — a Language of Life, by Marshall Roseberg
http://www.cnvc.org
http://www.nvctraining.com

Photographs

p.60. Maggie Nielson, 27 July 2006.

p.67. Corrie Wingate.

p.83. Fronteiras do Pensamento, 9 September 2012.

p.108. Jordi Bernabeu Farrús

p.147. Claude Truong-Ngoc, 22 October 2013.

Acknowledgements

This text has evolved from conversations with colleagues who have far more experience than I; people who have helped stop the Colombian civil war that has claimed more than 220,000 lives; people who have negotiated quietly to build an agreement between Iran and the USA over nuclear weapons production; people who risk their lives daily so that other people don't get killed in DR Congo, Nepal, Pakistan, Somalia, Sri Lanka, Sudan and Zimbabwe.

In particular I would like to thank HH the Dalai Lama for giving the book his full attention at the Mind and Life Conference in September 2016. Guy Lieberman and the FCB Foundation offered encouragement and initial design work. My gratitude also goes to all those who read versions of the text and made suggestions that have improved ideas and prevented mistakes, including John Paul Lederach, Gabrielle Rifkind, Dylan Mathews, Paul Ingram, Nicholas Janni, Simon Fisher, Guy Lieberman, Polly McAfee, Karen Downes, Kristina Lunz, Bea Benkova, Samantha Moyo, Elsie Bryant, Lawrence Kershen, Darshita Gillies, Al Jubitz, John Hamwee, Lawrence Bloom, David Hartsough, Daniel Danso, Kerstin Loeber Mark Rylance, Annie Lennox, Brian Eno and Professors Paul Rogers and Kalypso Nicolaidis. Emily Hutchinson helped prepare the photo-shoot. Paul Lock, Simon Henson and Nishant Malapatti helped with obtaining corporate responses to ways in which business could benefit from reductions in armed violence.

Lysan Boshuijzen added key points to the manuscript and worked tirelessly on printing arrangements, distribution and marketing. Kristina Lunz helped with research, and Eliza Cass updated the figures. Edward Elworthy and Roland Ward checked numbers. Steve Killelea, founder of the Institute for Economics and Peace — publishers of the Global Peace Index — was most helpful, as was Daniel Hyslop in checking and amending the unit costs in chapter 5 (while responsibility for the concepts naturally rests with the author).

I am also most appreciative of the Ammerdown Group for permission to use extracts from their excellent report *Rethinking Security: A discussion paper* published in 2016, and to Liz Kingsnorth for permission to use her Tips for Effective Communication.

Huge gratitude goes to Marianne Ryan, who generously offered her expertise and a great deal of her time to make editorial recommendations that have transformed the original text.

Ben Shmulevitch took enormous care with the entire design and style of presentation of the book, his patience was extraordinary, and his skill has made the layout and the diagrams communicate the facts in a clear effective way.

Finally I'm deeply grateful to Alexandra Feldner for her passion and commitment to the book and to discovering the right cover design, and to Pal Hansen for his incredible photographic skills to make this possible.

If you are especially moved by this book please make a donation to Peace Direct https://www.peacedirect.org/donate/ and or send copies to your friends.

By the same author:

1980 The Role of Women in Peace Movements, Peace Research and the Improvement of International Relations (UNESCO, Paris)

1986 Editor (as Scilla McLean): How Nuclear Weapons Decisions Are Made (Macmillan, London)

1987 Author: Who Decides? Accountability and Nuclear Weapons Decision-Making in Britain, (Oxford Research Group).

1988 Producer: The Nuclear Weapons World: Who How and Where (Pinter Publishers, London).

1989 Author: Parliament, the Public and NATO's Nuclear Weapons, (Oxford Research Group).

1990 Co-author: New Threats and New Responses: proposals for future security decision-making in Europe, (Oxford Research Group).

1991 Co-author: Defence and Security in the New Europe: Who will decide? (Oxford Research Group).

1996 Editor and contributor: Re-thinking Defence and Foreign Policy, (Spokesman Press, London).

1996 Author: 'Power & Sex' (Element Books).

1997 Editor: Proposals for a Nuclear Weapon-Free World – a meeting between China and the West (Oxford Research Group).

2001 Co-author: The United States, Europe and the Majority World after 11 September (Oxford Research Group).

2001 Author: The Widening Atlantic (Open Democracy).

2002 Co-author with Professor Paul Rogers: A Never-Ending War? Consequences of 11 September (Oxford Research Group).
2002 Co-author with Professor Paul Rogers: The 'War on Terrorism': 12-month audit and future strategy options (Oxford Research Group).

2003 Author: The crisis over Iraq: the non-military solution (Open Democracy).

2004 Author: Cutting the Costs of War: non-military prevention and resolution of conflict (Oxford Research Group).

2005 Author: Tackling Terror By Winning Hearts & Minds (Open Democracy).

2005 Co-author: Hearts and Minds: human security approaches to political violence (Demos, London).

2006 Author: If Diplomacy Fails (Open Democracy).

2006 Co-author with Gabrielle Rifkind: Making Terrorism History (Random House, London).

2009 Co-author with Anne Baring: Soul Power (Booksurge, USA).

2009 Author: Peace and Security Now, (Fetzer Institute, USA).

2010 Author: 'Tools for Peace' (World Peace Partnership).

2011 Author: 'Peace Begins with Me' (World Peace Partnership).

2014 Author: 'Pioneering the Possible: awakened leadership for a world that works' (North Atlantic Books).

Author

Scilla Elworthy PhD

Three times Nobel Peace Prize nominee for her work with Oxford Research Group to develop effective dialogue between nuclear weapons policy-makers worldwide and their critics, work which included a series of meetings between Chinese, Russian and western nuclear scientists and military. She founded Peace Direct in 2002 to fund, promote and learn from local peace-builders in conflict areas: Peace Direct was voted 'Best New Charity' in 2005.

Scilla was awarded the Niwano Peace Prize in 2003 and was adviser to Peter Gabriel, Archbishop Desmond Tutu, and Sir Richard Branson in setting up 'The Elders'. Scilla co-founded Rising Women Rising World in 2013, and FemmeQ in 2016 to establish the qualities of feminine intelligence for women and men as essential to use in building a safer world. Her TED talk on nonviolence has been viewed by over 1,130,000 people. Her latest book *The Business Plan for Peace: Building a World Without War* (2017) and her book *Pioneering the Possible – awakened leadership for a world that works* (North Atlantic Books, 2014) received critical acclaim from experts in the field.

Scilla is an Ambassador for Peace Direct, a Councillor of the World Future Council and patron of Oxford Research Group; adviser to the Syria Campaign and the Institute for Economics and Peace. She advises the leadership of selected international corporations as well as students and young social entrepreneurs. Scilla is a mother, stepmother, and grandmother and loves messing about in her garden near Oxford in the UK.